T0191773

QUANAH PARKER

NORTH AMERICAN INDIANS OF ACHIEVEMENT

QUANAH PARKER
Comanche Chief

Claire Wilson

Senior Consulting Editor
W. David Baird
Howard A. White Professor of History
Pepperdine University

CHELSEA HOUSE PUBLISHERS

New York   Philadelphia

FRONTISPIECE   An early portrait of Quanah Parker shows him regally dressed. At a young age, Quanah became skilled at raiding, through which he acquired many possessions.

ON THE COVER   An original painting from a photograph of Quanah Parker taken by Charles M. Bell, circa 1890.

Chelsea House Publishers
EDITOR-IN-CHIEF   Remmel Nunn
MANAGING EDITOR   Karyn Gullen Browne
COPY CHIEF   Mark Rifkin
PICTURE EDITOR   Adrian G. Allen
ART DIRECTOR   Maria Epes
ASSISTANT ART DIRECTOR   Noreen Romano
MANUFACTURING MANAGER   Gerald Levine
SYSTEMS MANAGER   Lindsey Ottman
PRODUCTION MANAGER   Joseph Romano
PRODUCTION COORDINATOR   Marie Claire Cebrián

North American Indians of Achievement
SENIOR EDITOR   Liz Sonneborn

Staff for QUANAH PARKER
ASSISTANT EDITOR   Brian Sookram
COPY EDITOR   Christopher Duffy
EDITORIAL ASSISTANT   Michele Haddad
DESIGNER   Debora Smith
PICTURE RESEARCHER   Vicky Haluska
COVER ILLUSTRATION   Daniel Mark Duffy

Copyright © 1992 by Chelsea House Publishers, a division of Main Line Book Co. All rights reserved. Printed and bound in Mexico.

First Printing

1   3   5   7   9   8   6   4   2

Library of Congress Cataloging-in-Publication Data

Wilson, Claire
Quanah Parker/by Claire Wilson
p. cm.
Includes bibliographical references and index.
Summary: Examines the life and career of the Comanche chieftain.
ISBN   0-7910-1702-8
1. Parker, Quanah, 1845?–1911. 2. Comanche Indians—Biography. 3. Comanche Indians—History. [1. Parker, Quanah. 1845?–1911. 2. Comanche Indians—Biography. 3. Indians of North America—Biography.] I. Title.
E99.C85P388 1991   91-10500
973'.0497402—dc20   CIP
[B]   AC

CONTENTS

NORTH AMERICAN INDIANS OF ACHIEVEMENT

Other titles in preparation

ON INDIAN LEADERSHIP

by W. David Baird

Howard A. White Professor of History

Pepperdine University

Authoritative utterance is in thy mouth, perception is in thy heart, and thy tongue is the shrine of justice," the ancient Egyptians said of their king. From him, the Egyptians expected authority, discretion, and just behavior. Homer's *Iliad* suggests that the Greeks demanded somewhat different qualities from their leaders: justice and judgment, wisdom and counsel, shrewdness and cunning, valor and action. It is not surprising that different people living at different times should seek different qualities from the individuals they looked to for guidance. By and large, a people's requirements for leadership are determined by two factors: their culture and the unique circumstances of the time and place in which they live.

Before the late 15th century, when non-Indians first journeyed to what is now North America, most Indian tribes were not ruled by a single person. Instead, there were village chiefs, clan headmen, peace chiefs, war chiefs, and a host of other types of leaders, each with his or her own specific duties. These influential people not only decided political matters but also helped shape their tribe's social, cultural, and religious life. Usually, Indian leaders held their positions because they had won the respect of their peers. Indeed, if a leader's followers at any time decided that he or she was out of step with the will of the people, they felt free to look to someone else for advice and direction.

Thus, the greatest achievers in traditional Indian communities were men and women of extraordinary talent. They were not only skilled at navigating the deadly waters of tribal politics and cultural customs but also able to, directly or indirectly, make a positive and significant difference in the daily life of their followers.

From the beginning of their interaction with Native Americans, non-Indians failed to understand these features of Indian leadership. Early European explorers and settlers merely assumed that Indians had the same relationship with their leaders as non-Indians had with their kings and queens. European monarchs generally inherited their positions and ruled large nations however they chose, often with little regard for the desires or needs of their subjects. As a result, the settlers of Jamestown saw Pocahontas as a "princess" and Pilgrims dubbed Wampanoag leader Metacom "King Philip," envisioning them in roles very different from those in which their own people placed them.

As more and more non-Indians flocked to North America, the nature of Indian leadership gradually began to change. Influential Indians no longer had to take on the often considerable burden of pleasing only their own people; they also had to develop a strategy of dealing with the non-Indian newcomers. In a rapidly changing world, new types of Indian role models with new ideas and talents continually emerged. Some were warriors; others were peacemakers. Some held political positions within their tribes; others were writers, artists, religious prophets, or athletes. Although the demands of Indian leadership altered from generation to generation, several factors that determined which Indian people became prominent in the centuries after first contact remained the same.

Certain personal characteristics distinguished these Indians of achievement. They were intelligent, imaginative, practical, daring, shrewd, uncompromising, and logical. They were constant in friendships, unrelenting in hatreds, affectionate with their relatives, and respectful to their God or gods. Of course, no single Native American leader embodied all these qualities, nor these qualities only. But it was these characteristics that allowed them to succeed.

The special skills and talents that certain Indians possessed also brought them to positions of importance. The life of Hiawatha, the legendary founder of the powerful Iroquois Confederacy, displays the value that oratorical ability had for many Indians in power. The biography of Cochise, the 19th-century Apache chief, illustrates that leadership often required keen diplomatic skills not only in transactions among tribespeople but also in hardheaded negotiations with non-Indians. For others, such as Mohawk Joseph Brant and Navajo Peter MacDonald, a non-Indian education proved advantageous in their dealings with other peoples.

Sudden changes in circumstance were another crucial factor in determining who became influential in Indian communities. King Philip in the 1670s and Geronimo in the 1880s both came to power when their people were searching for someone to lead them into battle against white frontiersmen who had forced upon them a long series of indignities. Seeing the rising discontent of Indians of many tribes in the 1810s, Tecumseh and his brother, the Shawnee prophet Tenskwatawa, proclaimed a message of cultural revitalization that appealed to thousands. Other Indian achievers recognized cooperation with non-Indians as the most advantageous path during their lifetime. Sarah Winnemucca in the late 19th century bridged the gap of understanding between her people and their non-Indian neighbors through the publication of her autobiography *Life Among the Piutes*. Olympian Jim Thorpe in the early 20th century championed the assimilationist policies of the U.S. government and, with his own successes, demonstrated the accomplishments Indians could make in the non-Indian world. And Wilma Mankiller, principal chief of the Cherokees, continues to fight successfully for the rights of her people through the courts and through negotiation with federal officials.

Leadership among Native Americans, just as among all other peoples, can be understood only in the context of culture and history. But the centuries that Indians have had to cope with invasions of foreigners in their homelands have brought unique hardships and obstacles to the Native American individuals who most influenced and inspired others. Despite these challenges, there has never been a lack of Indian men and women equal to these tasks. With such strong leaders, it is no wonder that Native Americans remain such a vital part of this nation's cultural landscape.

1

ANTELOPE WARRIORS

On a night in late September of 1871, a massive party of U.S. cavalry troops came together on the prairie at Clear Fork on the Brazos River in west Texas. The group, led by Colonel Ranald Mackenzie, consisted of 20 Indian scouts from the Tonkawa tribe and some 580 soldiers. These troops, the 4th Cavalry, were reputed to be one of the finest-trained regiments in the U.S. Army. However, they were extremely nervous because they were about to embark on a mission that not only had never been attempted before but the very idea of which created images of terror and death. Throughout that night and through the next few days, the group kept a constant—and tension-filled—watch along the horizon to their west. The troops were about to enter the Comanchería, homeland of the Comanche Indians.

Mackenzie and his men were searching for a particular group of Comanches—the Quahadis, or Antelope band. These Indians had been wreaking havoc on the Texas settlements that bordered their territory for almost 50 years and had fiercely resisted all efforts by the U.S. government to force them onto reservations. They did so even after every other Comanche group had been defeated and relocated. Instead of giving in, Quahadi war parties

Quanah Parker in a full-length headdress standing in front of a Comanche tipi. Quanah and his band, the Quahadis, terrorized Texas settlers throughout the 1860s.

had stepped up their retaliatory efforts as more and more farmsteads appeared on their ancient hunting grounds.

The successes of the Quahadis' attacks on white settlements and skirmishes with the cavalry were largely due to their great skill at guerrilla warfare and their in-depth knowledge of the landscape of the region. However, the driving force behind the Quahadis' unrelenting defense of their homeland lay in their greatest war leader—Kwanah. The son of Peta Nokona, a great Comanche leader, and Cynthia Ann Parker, a captured white settler, he is better known by the Americanized version of his name—Quanah Parker. A master tactician and a quick thinker, he easily second-guessed the plans of each U.S. Army expedition sent out against him.

The U.S. military and the Quahadis had several encounters before 1871, but these had been either chance meetings or retaliatory attacks. The Mackenzie force was the first concerted effort by the U.S. government to put an end to Comanche raiding. By this time, it had become imperative to the U.S. government that Quanah and his band be forced to move to the restrictive environment of a reservation.

The importance of this mission was made clear to Mackenzie by Lawrie Tatum, the federal representative at the Fort Sill reservation, in present-day Oklahoma. The reservation had been established for and was now home to the Kiowas, Kiowa-Apaches, and five Comanche bands. None of these peoples had moved willingly to the government lands, and none were particularly happy about the living conditions there. Tatum knew all too well that Quanah and the Quahadis had become almost legendary among the unhappy and belligerent reservation Indians. To them, the Quahadis symbolized the spirit of defiance and independence they hoped to regain. Tatum, Mackenzie, and the leadership of the U.S. Army realized that Texas would not be safe for white settlers until the Quahadis were disarmed and moved to the reservation.

There was good reason for the Fort Sill Indians to hold Quanah in such high regard. Such was his daring that, during Mackenzie's mustering activities at Clear Fork, he staged a raid only 20 miles from the soldiers' encampment. The Quahadi warriors got away with more than 100 cattle and more than 1,000 horses. This embarrassment was only one of what would become a long line of acts that would increase Mackenzie's determination to defeat and make prisoners of Quanah and his band.

On the day after the raid, Mackenzie ordered his troops to prepare to pursue the Quahadis and their prizes. With the Tonkawa scouts at the front, the force tracked the escaping Comanche warriors for the entire day without success. As night approached, the soldiers were forced to

A portion of the Brazos River, which flows from New Mexico through southern Texas. In 1871, the 4th Cavalry gathered, where Clear Fork wends into the Brazos River, to begin its assault on the Quahadis.

set up camp on the plains, placing themselves in an extremely vulnerable position. During the night, Quanah and his warriors stampeded a herd of buffalo straight through the soldiers' encampment.

The next morning, Mackenzie and his outfit again took up the chase. Later in the day, a few of the Tonkawa scouts discovered four Quahadi warriors spying on the troops' progress from the top of a hill. Quanah was keeping a close watch on Mackenzie's actions. The cavalry was as much the hunted as it was the hunter. Despite sighting the four Quahadi observers, Mackenzie was unable to make any headway toward capturing Quanah or regaining the stolen livestock.

Again Mackenzie was forced to make camp on the open plains. Again Quanah and his warriors took advantage of the soldiers' vulnerability. He and his men charged through the camp and took the sleeping soldiers completely by surprise. The Indians fired at the troops with rifles that they had obtained by trading stolen livestock. The war party headed directly for the soldiers' horses, stampeded them, and made off with more than 70 of them.

Quanah's tactics were well thought out and quite effective. As a result of his attack on the soldiers' camp, Colonel Mackenzie lost his temper and jumped to a hasty and regrettable decision. In his fury, he sent out a small party led by Lieutenant Robert Carter to pursue and attack the Quahadi war party and retake the stolen horses. This reaction proved to be exactly what Quanah wanted.

As soon as Carter and his troops had overtaken a group of fleeing Quahadis, they found themselves in the midst of an ambush. Quanah had used the small group of warriors to lure the cavalrymen into a canyon so that he could cut off any chance of their escape. The soldiers were forced to seek shelter in a break in the rocks and to keep

Colonel Ranald S. Mackenzie's ability and tenacity in fighting the Comanches won him the loyalty of his men.

firing incessantly to prevent the Comanche warriors from overwhelming them.

This attack gave rise to one of the earliest descriptions of Quanah Parker. Lieutenant Carter later wrote in his memoirs of his first sight of the war leader:

A large and powerfully built chief led the bunch on a coal-black racing pony. Leaning forward on his mane, his heels nervously working in the animal's side, with six-shooter poised in air, he seemed the incarnation of savage, brutal joy. His face was smeared with war paint, which gave his features a satanic look. A large, cruel mouth added to his ferocious appearance. A full-length warbonnet of eagle's feathers spread out as he rode, descending from his forehead and back to his pony's tail, almost sweeping the ground. Large brass hoops were in his ears. He was naked to the waist, wearing simply leggings, moccasins, and a breechclout. A necklace of bear's claws hung about his neck. His scalp lock [a special braid worn by many Plains warriors] was carefully braided with otter fur and tied with bright red flannel.

Carter's description is surely colored by his conception of American Indians as warlike savages and his desire to add drama to his own life story. However, it does provide valuable information about Quanah's appearance during a battle.

Carter and his small group of soldiers would most likely have been killed if Colonel Mackenzie had not come to their rescue with a large party of men. The cavalry drove off Quanah and his warriors and regrouped to continue the chase. Mackenzie sent out the Tonkawa scouts to determine the Comanches' direction of travel. Then, his entire force charged off after them, only to find the remains of the Indians' recently evacuated camp.

Mackenzie and his men quickly found that pursuit would not be an easy task. Quanah was leading his band on a circuitous and often overlapping trail in an effort to confuse Mackenzie. Also, the Comanches traveled along steep cliff faces and up hills, which posed no difficulty to the Indians' small and sure-footed ponies. For the large, stocky cavalry horses, however, the terrain was much harder to cross. Nevertheless, Mackenzie was determined to capture—or wipe out—his quarry, and he continued to follow as best he could. Still, the distance between the two groups was increasing as time passed.

As Mackenzie continued his pursuit of the retreating Comanches, he soon realized where they were headed—the Llano Estacado, or Staked Plain. No U.S. military

This lance and eagle-feather warbonnet belonged to Quanah. They were integral components of his battle gear.

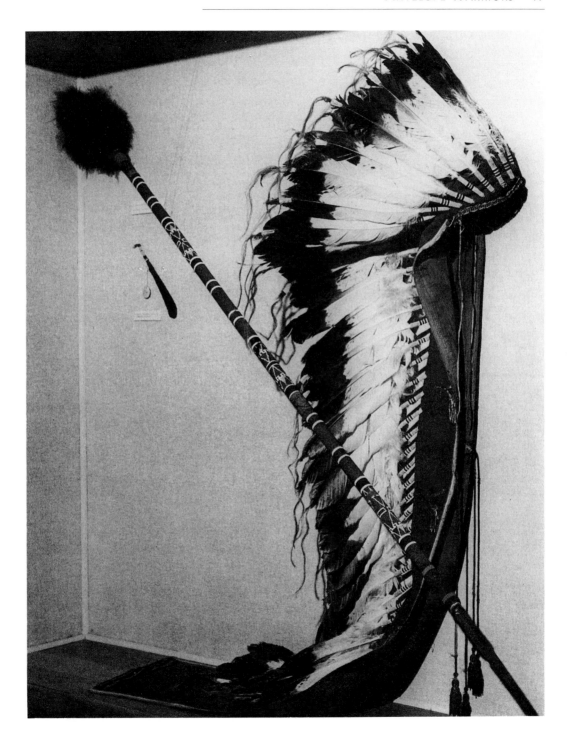

force had ever penetrated that ancient Indian homeland before, but Mackenzie did not stop to contemplate the historical significance of his actions. He merely did what his duty required of him.

After entering the Llano Estacado, the cavalrymen found that the Comanches' trail was littered with belongings that had been discarded in order to lighten their ponies' loads. By doing this, Quanah and his people were able to gain an even wider lead on Mackenzie and his troops. Yet, the soldiers doggedly followed the Quahadis throughout that day, but they were unable to close the gap. Even more aggravating, several of Quanah's warriors rode alongside the cavalry just out of rifle range but close enough to get off a few warning shots with their own weapons.

As night approached, the situation grew even worse for the U.S. troops. In early autumn, weather conditions in the region could shift without the slightest warning, making the season a particularly treacherous time on the Great Plains. Suddenly, high winds and snow showers hit the troops, and they quickly found themselves amidst snowdrifts of several inches. Their horses, already weary from following the Quahadis' arduous escape route, could no longer continue the pursuit. Reluctantly, Mackenzie decided to make camp for the evening.

Just as the cavalrymen were bedding down for a night of uneasy sleep, gunfire and Comanche war cries rang out. Quanah and his warriors had lived on the Llano Estacado all their life, so they were accustomed to the foul weather. The Quahadis rode straight through the camp firing indiscriminately into supply wagons and firepits. Then, as abruptly as they had appeared, Quanah and his men were gone. The soldiers were left to spend the remainder of the night staring nervously into the dark.

The coming of morning brought no relief from the miserable weather. It continued to snow and rain with no letup. Mackenzie was forced to concede defeat to Quanah and his warriors. With his worn-out troops, the colonel turned back toward Fort Richardson. Through all 509 miles of territory that they had covered in pursuit of Quanah and his Quahadi band, the U.S. troops had inflicted no perceptible harm on the Indians. Even though the Llano Estacado had been invaded for the first time, the U.S. government was still no closer to ending the Indian rampages on the Great Plains. The Quahadis and their clever leader were still free.

2

THE SNAKE PEOPLE

To better understand Quanah's bitter and relentless struggle to defend his people's land, it is helpful to trace the history of the Comanche people and their home—the Comanchería. The story of these Indians, however, does not begin on the Great Plains. It starts some 300 years ago in a region of the Rocky Mountains northwest of the Plains. At that time, the Comanches did not exist as a distinct cultural group. Instead, they comprised the southernmost groups of the Shoshone tribe, a mountain people who inhabited an area that extended across present-day Wyoming, Idaho, northeastern Nevada, western Kansas, small portions of Utah, and parts of western Montana.

The Comanches and the Shoshones then made up a single society with common customs and beliefs. These Indians referred to themselves as Nermernuh or Nerm, meaning "the People." Other nearby groups called them the Snake People. Even after the Comanches moved onto the Plains, other tribes continued to call them Snake Indians.

Most Plains tribes could not understand one another's language. In order to pass on information during trading or intertribal meetings, they developed a series of hand signs similar to today's sign language for the deaf. The

A Shoshone camp in Wind River Mountains, Wyoming, photographed by William Henry Jackson in 1870. The southernmost groups of the Shoshones migrated south and became known as the Comanches.

sign for the Comanches was made by moving one hand in a backward, wriggling motion that imitated the sinuous movements of a snake. According to Quanah Parker this sign arose because, during the migration to the Plains, a group of Comanches decided to turn back. The band leader chastised them and likened them to a snake moving backward.

Even after the Comanches separated from the Shoshones, they maintained a trading alliance and continued to share many cultural practices, including religious beliefs, family structure, and political organization. Some of the northern Comanche groups actually had more contact with their Shoshone relatives than with the Comanche bands far to the south. To this day, the two peoples still maintain a close relationship and speak languages so similar that they are mutually intelligible.

It is not clear why the Comanches migrated south. Possibly they wanted to avoid tribes to the east, such as the Crows and the Sioux, who were increasingly raiding and hunting in Shoshone territory. The Crows and the Sioux were part of a trade network that brought them guns and ammunition from Great Lakes peoples, who obtained these goods from French traders in exchange for furs.

The Comanche migration did not take place all at once. Instead, small bands (distinct cultural groups made up of several families) moved onto the Plains over several decades. The first bands probably began their southward route sometime in the late 17th century. The first written reference to the Comanches on the Great Plains was made by Spanish officials in 1705. By that time, several Comanche bands were already well established in their new home.

The migrating Comanches settled into five major regional divisions. Scholars believe that the first sig-

COMANCHE BAND LOCATIONS ON THE COMANCHERÍA 1750–1840

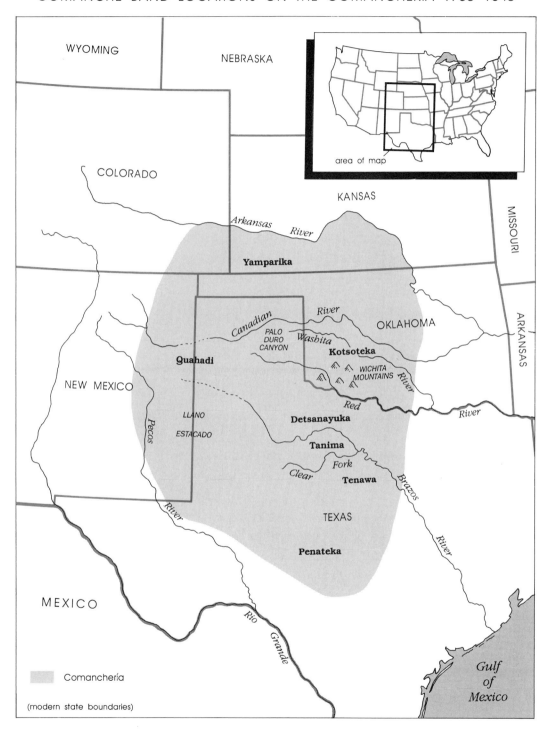

area of map

WYOMING

NEBRASKA

COLORADO

KANSAS

MISSOURI

Arkansas River

Yamparika

ARKANSAS

Canadian River

OKLAHOMA

PALO DURO CANYON

Washita

Kotsoteka

Quahadi

WICHITA MOUNTAINS

NEW MEXICO

Red River

River

LLANO ESTACADO

Detsanayuka

Pecos

Tanima

Clear Fork

Tenawa

Brazos River

TEXAS

Penateka

MEXICO

River

Rio Grande

Gulf of Mexico

Comanchería

(modern state boundaries)

nificant Comanche group to move onto the Plains was the Penatekas, or Honey Eaters. This band lived in the southeasternmost portion of the Comanchería and had the most frequent contact with non-Indian settlements there. They were also known as the Hois (Timber People), because of their proximity to the forests of what is now east Texas, and the Penanes (Wasps), because they were deadly quick during raids.

The region directly to the north of the Penatekas was inhabited by three bands called the Middle Comanches. They were the Tenawas (Downstream People), the Tanimas (Liver Eaters), and the Detsanayukas (Wanderers Who Make Bad Camps). This last group had earlier been called the Nokonis (Those Who Turn Back), after the name of their leader. When he died, the group was forced to change its name because Comanche tradition forbade even the mention of a deceased person's name. The Nokonis came by their new name because they relocated much more often than other Comanche bands and, in the opinion of these other groups, did not take the time to set up proper camps.

North of the Middle Comanches were the Kotsotekas, the Buffalo Eaters. Although all Comanches ate buffalo meat, this band lived in a region that was particularly rich in these animals. During the 17th and 18th centuries, the Kotsotekas were very active in trade with the Spanish.

At the most northerly reaches of the Comanchería lived the Yamparikas, or Root Eaters. This band's name came from the Shoshone custom of eating the roots of the yampa plant, also known as the Indian potato.

To the southwest of the Yamparikas lived the Quahadis, the Antelope band. They were named after this animal because they inhabited the flat, treeless prairies of the Llano Estacado, in which antelope were plentiful. Although this band was very populous, it did not become

Two Indians of the Ute tribe, which had settled on the southern Plains before the Comanches arrived there. The Comanches apparently got their name from the Ute word Koh-mats. *This word was recorded by the Spanish as* Komantcia *and later translated by the Americans as* Comanche.

well known among non-Indians until the late 19th century.

When the five divisions of the Comanche tribe moved onto the southern Great Plains, they did not simply pick out camps, set up villages, and settle down to a daily routine. Unfortunately for the Comanches, other tribes—such as the Apaches, the Osages, the Tonkawas, and the Utes—had discovered the benefits of the southern Plains long before the Comanches got there. So before this tribe could call the territory home, they had to rid it of its current occupants.

Had the Comanches been a people who traveled on foot and carried their belongings on their backs or on the backs of their dogs, this task might have proved impossible. However, a significant battle during the late 17th century indirectly allowed the Comanches to become one of the most powerful tribes in the region. The conflict was between a group of Indians and the Spanish missionaries and soldiers who had enslaved them.

A drawing of Don Juan de Oñate, the Spanish explorer. Oñate established settlements among the Pueblo Indians in what is now New Mexico.

The events leading to the incident began in 1598, when Spanish conquistador Don Juan de Oñate led an expedition north from Mexico into what is now New Mexico. His purpose was to establish a garrison and mission among the Indians who lived there along the Rio Grande. These Indians had farming communities where they raised corn, beans, squash, and cotton. They lived in adobe buildings (structures made of sun-dried earth and straw) that the Spanish called pueblos, so they became known as Pueblo Indians.

Oñate and his party settled among the Pueblo people, built their own adobe structures, planted fields, and fenced in grazing land for their livestock. They freely used the Pueblos' land and water. Soon, they also began to enslave the Indians. Through threats and harsh punishments, the Spanish forced the Pueblos to work their farms. However, the Pueblos' labor was not enough. The Spanish also established missions and exerted the same sort of pressure to convert the Indians to Roman Catholicism.

The Pueblos suffered under Spanish domination for 90 years, during which time they attempted several unsuccessful revolts. But in August of 1680, the Pueblos finally launched a concerted and full-scale attack against their overlords. The Spanish, taken by surprise at the sheer number of Indian rebels, fled rapidly from their ranches and farms, leaving behind all but their most valued possessions.

To the Indians, few of the Spaniards' luxury furnishings and trappings were of any use. However, one type of Spanish possession was of great interest—their horses. When the Pueblos were under Spanish control, they were forbidden to own or even to ride a horse. The Europeans knew that mounted Indians would be hard to control, so they kept a tight grip on their horses. However, the Spanish gentry were willing to retain Indians as stablehands. Thus, many learned everything they needed to know about the care and breeding of these animals. After the Indians' successful battle, now known as the Pueblo Revolt, they soon mastered the technique of riding.

The Pueblos also quickly learned the horse's value as a trade item. In less than a decade, the horse trade penetrated into regions hundreds of miles to the north, east, and west of the Pueblo homeland. Included in this vast trade network were the Nermernuh people, whose migration onto the southern Plains was made much faster after their acquisition of horses. By the beginning of the 18th century, the mountain Shoshones possessed hundreds of horses, as did the branch of this tribe that became the Comanches.

During the next several decades, Comanche warriors drove the inhabitants of the southern Plains out of the region. In the eastern portion of what was to become the Comanchería, they mounted raids against the Pawnees and Wichitas; to the southwest, against the Navajos; and to the north, against the Utes.

The most brutal and devastating of these attacks, however, were waged against the Apaches. These people hunted buffalo and also maintained settled farming communities in what are now southeastern New Mexico and western Texas. The Apaches posed an easy target. Unlike the other tribes, who lived for the most part in mobile hunting camps, they were tied to their fields and

thus simple to locate. By 1750, the land once occupied by the Apaches had become the major portion of the Comanchería.

After the Comanches were firmly in control of their territory, their possession of horses helped them to flourish. The area had an abundant supply of game, including buffalo, as well as nuts, tubers, fruits, and other wild foods. And because the Comanches defended their land unrelentingly, there was rarely any competition for these necessities. On horseback, the Indians could travel farther to hunt or raid and could carry back heavy loads of food supplies and other needed goods. This situation

Pueblo Indians planting corn. They were an agricultural people who wove cloth and made baskets. After overthrowing their Spanish masters, the Pueblos engaged in the horse trade.

allowed the Comanche population to swell to an all-time high of approximately 20,000 during the mid-18th century.

Not only was the living easier on the southern Plains, the opportunities for acquiring goods were better, too. After the Comanches succeeded in driving the Apaches from their villages, the way was open for direct trade with Europeans. With the Spanish of New Mexico, the Comanches traded dried meat, buffalo skins, and Indian captives (used by the Spanish as servants and farmhands) for metal tools and weapons. However, the Spanish refused to provide the Comanches with either guns or ammunition. They realized that the Indians would most likely use these weapons against Spanish settlers.

The Comanches were able to procure guns from another group of Europeans—the French, who were competing with the Spanish for possession of southwestern North America. The Comanches also provided the French traders with Indian captives (usually Apaches) and buffalo skins. Because the French had few troops in the region, it was to their advantage to encourage the Comanches and other tribes to continue fighting with the Spanish. The French had no settlements in Comanche territory and therefore had little reason to fear arming the Indians. They also realized that the Indians could not repair their weapons or manufacture the ammunition themselves. The Indians would therefore be obliged to remain on friendly terms with the French.

Even with French-supplied guns, the Comanches' relationship with the New Mexico Spanish during the 18th century was characterized by alternating periods of peace and war. Peace was usually made for the short term by small trading parties, who saw war as an obstacle to their acquisition of goods. The Comanches could not, however, make any trading alliances with the Spaniards in Texas, no matter how badly they might have needed their goods. A Comanche attack on the San Saba mission near San Antonio in 1758 had forever barred the way for trade between the two groups.

The unstable relationship between the Comanches and their trading partners existed, for the most part, because of the loose social organization of the various Comanche bands. If one Comanche group established a peaceful trading alliance with a Spanish village, it in no way meant that any other band had to honor the agreement, nor did it mean that that Comanche group would refrain from attacking other Spanish villages. There was no tribal body of law. This was a major difference between the culture of the Comanches and that of the Europeans who tried to control them. It would also eventually be a major factor in the Indians' downfall.

During the 1760s, the political climate of southwestern North America began to change. To the east, the French and British were waging the French and Indian War. In 1763, the conflict ended with France's defeat. As a result, the French were forced to give up their holdings in North America. The Spanish then took charge of the territory claimed by France on the eastern border of the Comanchería. Now the Comanches were surrounded on three sides by the Spaniards.

The Spanish soon took advantage of the situation. In 1779, Spanish official Juan Bautista de Anza and his troops attacked and defeated a large Comanche village in the northern part of the Comanchería. Things worsened for the Indians in 1780 and 1781 when a smallpox epidemic broke out, killing many tribe members.

These blows, combined with a fear of further attacks from the heavily armed Spanish troops, drove bands of Comanches in the west to agree to an action that was unheard of in their culture. In 1786, a contingent of war

A portrait of Don Juan Bautista de Anza, who led a Spanish contingent that defeated the Comanches in the northern part of the Comanchería in 1779.

and civil leaders met with de Anza in Taos, New Mexico, and grudgingly conceded to his demand that they choose one leader to represent them all. The Indians selected Ecueracapa (Leather Jacket), a prominent war leader. Ecueracapa made a pact to stop attacks on Spanish settlements in New Mexico in return for uninterrupted trade and the Spaniards' assistance in Comanche raids against the Apaches. An alliance was thereby created between the Comanches and the New Mexico traders— who were known as Comancheros—that would last well into the 20th century.

As the 18th century came to a close, Spain's hold over southwestern North America began to wane and Comanche power began to rise. These changes occurred because of Spain's involvement in several European wars. These conflicts left the Spanish with less money and military personnel to maintain their landholdings thousands of miles away. As a result, the Comanches were able to increase both the number and extent of their raids. The Spanish settlers in Texas and northern Mexico were hardest hit because they had never made any peace agreement with the Comanches.

The Comanche raids into these two areas continued unchecked throughout the first three decades of the 19th century despite two major political upheavals in the region. The first event was the United States's purchase of Louisiana Territory from France in 1803. (This land had been reacquired by France in accordance with the Treaty of San Ildefonso in 1800.) This vast tract, which stretched from the Mississippi River to the Rocky Mountains, included the Comanchería. The purchase at first had little effect on the Comanches other than to introduce them to American traders, who now began to travel the trade routes with the French and Spanish traders. Some of the traders' wagon trains were crossing the

Comanchería, especially those traveling from St. Louis to Santa Fe, but these trips posed no direct threat to Comanche land.

The second event was Mexico's 1821 victory in its war for independence from Spain. However, the Mexicans were in the same position as the Spanish had been, having neither the funds nor the manpower to tackle the Comanches. Because of their military inadequacy, the Mexicans conceived of a different type of plan to keep the Comanches from raiding their villages. Soon after independence, Mexico began to allow a few American families to settle in their Texas colony.

Those few quickly swelled to several thousand, which was exactly what the Mexicans had hoped would happen. They were willing to give up some of their territory (which they could not defend anyway) with the expectation that the Americans would act as a barrier between

Plains Indians attacking a wagon train. The Americans would ultimately subdue the Indians mainly because of their superior military might.

themselves and the raiding Comanches. However, most of the settlers established their farms far to the east of Comanche raiding trails into Mexico, so they went largely unnoticed by the warriors for more than 10 years.

Beginning in 1830, new changes began to occur on the southern Plains. This time, the Comanches were directly threatened. In that year, President Andrew Jackson pushed through Congress a bill that would allow him to negotiate for the "removal," or relocation, of Indian tribes in the eastern United States to lands west of the Mississippi River. As a result of this legislation, known as the Indian Removal Act, the Cherokees, Choctaws, Creeks, Chickasaws, and Seminoles were coerced to resettle in what is now eastern Oklahoma, then part of a larger tract known as Indian Territory.

But these lands were already inhabited by other tribes, such as the Wichitas and the Osages. When the eastern Indians arrived in Indian Territory, they forced these other groups to move westward in search of game—Comanche game. Understandably, hostilities erupted between the Comanches and their encroaching neighbors, as well as between these displaced tribes and the eastern Indians. This warfare drove the U.S. government to send a representative, Sam Houston, to meet with some of the Wichitas and Comanches in 1832, resulting in a nominal peace treaty.

At about the same time, settlers from Texas began to move onto Comanche territory from the southeast. Their settlements were almost irresistible to Comanche raiders because, unlike the clustered ranches and pueblos of the Mexicans, American farmsteads were few, widely separated, and virtually undefendable. The Comanches began raiding Texan homesteads sometime in 1835, and they were tacitly encouraged by the Texas government's inability to retaliate.

Sam Houston was one of the few U.S. government officials who sought fair treatment for the Comanches. He served twice as president of the Republic of Texas and was governor of the state of Texas from 1859 to 1861.

The Texans were unable to send any troops after Comanche raiders because they were embroiled in a battle with Mexico for their independence. They achieved their goal and became a sovereign country—the Republic of Texas—in 1836, at which time they turned their attention toward the Indian raiders. Unexpectedly, Sam Houston, the president of the republic, argued for a peaceable solution. He had spent many years among the Cherokees and had an understanding of the way the Indians viewed land ownership. Houston sent officials to negotiate peace with the Indians, promising to set up trade networks with them. But his views were not supported by the Texas senate, which refused to ratify his agreements.

During the remainder of the 1830s and well into the 1840s, warfare steadily increased. As more settlers moved into Texas, more Comanche raiding parties attacked them and more Texas military groups, known as Rangers, pursued and battled the Comanches. Into this world of continual warfare and of unbridled hostility between differing cultures, Quanah was born among the Detsanayukas to Cynthia Ann Parker and Peta Nokona.

This woodcut shows some sur-
vivors of the Fort Parker mas-
sacre preparing to eat a
skunk. After the Indians at-
tacked the fort, the occupants
were fearful that they might
return and did not venture out
for several days.

3

THE SERPENT EAGLE

On May 19, 1836, a Comanche raiding party, accompanied by several Wichita, Kiowa, and Caddo warriors, came upon a large stockade that had been settled two years earlier by the Parker family. The fort was located on the floodplain of the Navostos River in east central Texas and was now home to 6 families, totaling approximately 30 people. As the riders approached the gate, one of the men inside the fort came out to see what they wanted. The leader asked the settler for the location of a place to water the warriors' horses and for a steer for them to eat.

Unaware of his danger, the settler refused. The warriors quickly killed him and forced their way into the stockade, killing all the men that they came upon and taking captive several of the women and children. However, a group of armed settlers, who had been working in nearby fields, rushed back to the fort and managed to free two of the captives. The warriors raced off, taking with them Elizabeth Kellogg, Rachel Plummer, Plummer's infant son James, and two of the Parker children—John and Cynthia Ann.

When they were a safe distance from the settlement, the war party split up. The Caddos and Wichitas went north, taking Elizabeth Kellogg with them. The Comanches and Kiowas headed west with the rest of the captives. They took their prizes back to the encampment of the Detsanayuka Comanche band, where they were divided among several of the families.

In the months that followed, the three white children were adopted into the band and treated as members of the tribe. Plummer, however, was treated as a slave. Her captors abused her terribly until she retaliated against one of the tribeswomen who had been trying to beat her. The Comanche who owned Plummer was so impressed by her assertive act that he allowed her to assume the role of a tribe member. Not long afterward, however, she was discovered by a non-Indian trader, ransomed, and returned to her family. But Plummer was not welcomed back as she might have liked. Because she had spent so much time among "savages," she was no longer considered fit for life in white society and was shunned by her family and friends. As a result, Plummer's health declined rapidly during the months after her "rescue." She died early in 1838.

By contrast, the three children thrived among their adoptive families. They had become full-fledged Comanches and were treated no differently than any of the tribe's other children. All were taught the beliefs and customs of the tribe with the expectation that they would grow up to be productive members of the society. However, the children's location was discovered in 1842 by white traders, and negotiations for their return were soon begun. After some deliberation, James Plummer and John Parker were ransomed and returned to their families.

Cynthia Ann, however, had become fully assimilated into Comanche life and would not leave. She was seen on several occasions by Americans in the region, but all attempts to secure her return ended in failure. Most of

Drawing of a Comanche village by George Catlin in 1836. The women at right are drying buffalo hides while the men, at left, are playing a game.

the men who met with her stated that she would not speak to them in English, responded only to her Comanche name (Naduah), and showed no desire to return to her family. In time, except for her blue eyes, she would look like any other Indian who lived on the Plains.

Around 1845, at the age of 18, Naduah married Peta Nokona. Together they had three children. They called their first-born Quanah, which means Fragrant. Although historical accounts vary as to Quanah's year of birth, most sources agree that it was about 1845. His brother, Pecos (Peanut), was born two years later. And several years after, Naduah gave birth to a girl, whom she named Topsannah (Flower).

When Cynthia Ann Parker became Naduah, she was schooled in the many activities and skills that would be required of her as a Comanche wife. Except for the heaviest work, she was responsible for all of the daily chores in her family's encampment. She prepared and

A buckskin dress. Among their other duties, Comanche women were responsible for making all clothing for their family.

cooked all of the food, made and repaired tools, clothing, bedding, and tipi covers, and packed and unpacked the family's belongings when her band changed locations.

The bulk of Naduah's day was spent preparing her family's food, which was obtained from a variety of sources. The Comanchería was a rich environment, and the Indians took full advantage of its diverse resources. Plentiful supplies of water, game, fruits, vegetables, medicinal plants, and the raw materials for tools and utensils were easy to find.

Various forms of the parfleche. *These rawhide bags were used to store food.*

The most important food resource was the buffalo, but the Comanches also hunted many other types of game, such as antelope, deer, and elk. The Indians sometimes even butchered their horses and mules if no other meat was available. Peta Nokona and the other Comanche hunters would take care of the primary butchering of game animals, but when they were finished, the women would complete the rest of the necessary preparations. All Comanches, except for the very young and the very old, took part in major hunts.

After the hunting party brought the meat back to camp, the majority of it was dried for storage. Comanche women dried meat by hanging strips of it over wooden poles that were suspended above a smoky fire. They also mixed pounded dried meat with melted fat, nuts, and fruit (such as cherries or plums) and stored the mixture in the stomach or intestines of a buffalo. This dish, known as *pemmican*, was a much sought after delicacy among non-Indians in the region.

Some of the meat was cooked immediately to celebrate the successful hunt. Before the Comanches acquired metal pots from non-Indian traders, they would skewer chunks of meat with wooden stakes and then either hold or prop up the stakes over an open fire. When the meat was roasted, a Comanche woman would simply remove the skewers from the fire and serve the meat, after placing it on a stiff animal hide. Sometimes she would cover the meat with a gravy made from honey, water, and animal bone marrow.

When Cynthia Ann Parker came to live among the Comanches, they had been using metal cookware for some time. Consequently, food preparation was much easier— Naduah merely kept stews cooking in pots throughout the day. In this way, her sons and husband could just dip into the hot, rich broth with a sharp stick, a knife, or even a bare hand and scoop out chunks of stewed meat. Comanche women often flavored such stews with wild onions.

Aside from hunts for game, Naduah and other Comanche women also went on expeditions to gather vegetables and fruits. From the many trees on the Comanchería, they gathered hickory nuts, piñon nuts, and acorns, as well as mulberries, plums, and persimmons. Likewise, they collected fruit from prickly pear cacti. They pounded these fruits into meal, which was then

Comanche woman erecting a tipi in the 1890s. Four sturdy poles provided the main support for the buffalo-skin covering that was fastened over the framework.

shaped into cakes and dried for consumption in winter. Naduah also dug up the tuberous roots of the yampa plant, wild onion, and Jerusalem artichoke.

The Comanches did not have any set mealtimes during the day. However, Naduah, Peta Nokona, and their children would eat together in the morning and in the evening. Before they began a meal, Peta Nokona would offer the first bit of food to the mythological creator of the Comanches, whom non-Indians refer to as the Great Spirit. It was common for Peta Nokona to have several guests because the Comanches believed that hospitality was extremely important. As one Comanche man named Slope noted, "Meat is free to those who come. [The Comanches] never got tired of visitors."

The buffalo was the source of most of the everyday objects used by Naduah and her family, as well as the rest of the Comanches. From some of the tanned hides, Naduah fashioned clothing for herself, her husband, and her children. Peta Nokona and his sons, after they had reached adolescence, dressed in buckskin shirts, leggings, moccasins, and breechcloths. A breechcloth consisted of a piece of buckskin that was passed between the legs and hung over a belt at the front and back. Naduah dressed in a buckskin dress, leggings, and moccasins. The infant Topsannah was wrapped in soft rabbit skin and placed in a cradleboard—a flat piece of wood on which a baby was securely fastened with rawhide thongs. All of the family's clothing was decorated with rawhide fringe and painted designs. Unlike many other Plains tribes, however, the Comanches ascribed no special meaning to these painted symbols; they were simply decoration.

Naduah also used buffalo hide to make the dwelling in which she and her family kept their belongings. A typical tipi consisted of some 10 to 20 buffalo hides that had been scraped, tanned, and sewn together. This cover was then fastened over a framework of approximately 20 wooden poles. Four of these poles were particularly sturdy and made up the main skeleton of the dwelling. The others were spaced out around the circumference to provide even support for the skin covering. Early non-Indian travelers reported that these dwellings were much warmer and more water resistant than the wooden or sod shacks erected by settlers. Tipis were also much easier to set up, usually taking no more than 20 minutes.

Inside his tipi, Peta Nokona placed his bed—which he shared with Naduah—opposite the door, a place that honored his position as head of the family. Quanah and Pecos kept their beds on either side. Topsannah slept between her parents, as did most Comanche infants until they were able to walk. The family's belongings filled the spaces between the beds, and a fireplace took up the center of the structure. From the poles, the family also hung stores of dried meat and fruit that were kept in *parfleches*—rawhide bags that resembled large envelopes.

In Comanche society, tipis were used for different purposes, such as sickroom, relaxation room, and meeting room. However, contrary to what is normally believed, the Comanches did not always sleep in their tipis. For much of the year, the weather on the Great Plains was warm enough for most Comanches to sleep under simple brush shelters. These consisted of four poles that supported a roof of leafy branches. The structure kept the Indians dry if it rained but allowed cool breezes to enter on all four sides. Only during the coldest months did a Comanche family spend the night in its tipi.

Even though Naduah did all of the work required to erect and take down her family's tipi, it was the property of her husband. For the most part, men were in control of Comanche society, but no one Comanche man had any more or less power over any other. For example, Peta

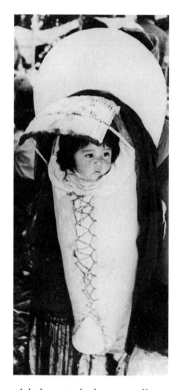

A baby attached to a cradle-board strapped to its mother's back. By using the cradle-board, a woman could ensure that her child was safe while she went about her daily chores.

Nokona was a great leader of the Detsanayuka Comanche band, but this was only because of his skill. He was not elected to the post nor could he be. He was only able to persuade other warriors to join a hunting or war party by virtue of his past successes. He could never force anyone to join.

Leaders such as Peta Nokona most often organized war parties to steal horses, supplies, and weapons; intimidate would-be trespassers; retaliate against enemy attacks; and acquire captives. Performing such aggressive activities was one of the few ways for a Comanche to gain status. Each warrior could retain his exalted position in the band by repeatedly proving his skills. Another way to achieve stature was to exhibit an ability to contact and use the power of the supernatural world. A man or woman who could do this might be given the title of *puhakut*, or medicine man.

During Quanah's youth, because the Comanches were almost perpetually at war, their everyday political and social decisions were made by a group of high-ranking warriors. In past times, these matters had been overseen by male elders who headed the families in each band. However, in the 1830s and 1840s, when virtually every determination centered on warfare or retaliatory raiding, the elders and the warriors joined together in the decision making.

When the leaders came together to make important judgments, one of the men was usually singled out to direct the meeting. This man would most likely be chosen because he had lived through many difficulties and would therefore know the best ways to deal with them. To this individual, non-Indians most commonly, and incorrectly, applied the term *chief*, particularly when the man was the spokesperson for his band in meetings with non-Indians. For example, Peta Nokona was known among non-Indians as a Comanche chief, but his Detsanayuka band had endowed him with no such authority.

Leaders such as Peta Nokona served only as a source of opinion, not of law. They could not impose their will on the rest of the band. The only weight that their decisions held was the weight of experience. As a Comanche named That's It said of the band leaders, "No one made [them] such; [they] just got that way."

Many years of training and participation in military and social activities were necessary to achieve the status accorded to Peta Nokona and other Comanche leaders. In childhood, all Comanches were generally treated as equals (although the birth of a boy was usually a greater cause for celebration). Only after a child began to participate actively in everyday Comanche society could his or her status grow.

Buffalo hunting was an important component of the Indians' way of life. These animals were a source of food, clothing, and shelter. For a Comanche male, a buffalo kill was also a significant rite of passage.

When Quanah was born, he entered the world in a special birth hut. Here, Naduah remained for several days after she delivered him. When she was able to leave the birth hut and resume her usual activities, she kept Quanah with her at all times. In typical Comanche fashion, she carried her baby in a cradleboard. With the infant Quanah secured inside this device, Naduah could either strap him to her back like a backpack or prop him up against a tipi wall or a tree. In this way, he was kept out of harm's way and was always within easy reach of his mother.

Quanah's training as a future Comanche warrior did not begin until he learned to walk. His first task was to master horseback riding, a skill that was most important to the Comanches' way of life on the Great Plains. There was no shortage of horses on which to train because, like most prominent warriors, Peta Nokona owned several hundred, perhaps even a thousand.

At first, Quanah was only allowed to ride with another person. However, as his skills developed, he was permitted to have a small pony of his own. He then progressed to riding bareback on more feisty animals and soon became adept at acquiring and maintaining his own herd. As Quanah would come to learn, most of a Comanche man's day was spent on horseback: either raiding, fighting, hunting, or moving camp. Therefore, a man who could not ride well was at best a hindrance to the band and at worst a danger to it.

When Quanah was not busy practicing horsemanship, he was learning about all the other things that he would need to know as an adult. In Comanche society, it was customary for a boy to learn from his mother's father. Because this was not possible in Quanah's case, he most likely received much of his instruction from his paternal grandfather, the great war leader Pohebits Quasho.

Quanah also spent time training with his father and, probably, his father's brothers. (There are few records of this period of Quanah's life.)

These men taught him how to use a bow and arrow and a lance, to track game on the many trails of the Comanchería, and to ride both defensively and offensively. Contemporary observers have remarked that the Comanches were among the finest riders in North America. George Catlin, an American artist who traveled among the Plains tribes in the early 19th century, noted: "Every young man . . . is able to drop his body upon the side of his horse . . . effectually screened from his enemies' weapons as he lays in a horizontal position. He will hang whilst his horse is at fullest speed, carrying with him his bow and his shield, and also his lance."

Comanche warriors were particularly adept at horsemanship. This rider has dropped to the side of his horse, effectively screening himself from his enemies' weapons.

Pohebits Quasho also passed on to Quanah the history of the Comanche people, including their rituals, their songs, and most important, their code of conduct. The Comanches had no written laws, nor offices or institutions that could enforce them. As Quanah learned while growing up, punishment for wrongdoing usually entailed being subjected to the scorn and ridicule of fellow band members. Because the Comanches were a very social people who needed each other to survive, this type of punishment was more than sufficient to keep even the most rebellious of adolescents in line.

When Quanah reached adolescence, he had to undergo three rites of passage, as did most Comanche boys. The first required him to move from his family's tipi into a tipi of his own. He did this because, according to Comanche custom, he could not inhabit the same dwelling as his sister, Topsannah. The second rite was Quanah's first buffalo hunt. Unless the boy was able to make a kill, he was not considered a man and, consequently, could not accompany the warriors during raids.

After Quanah achieved his first kill during a hunt, he had to undergo the third rite of passage—a vision quest—before he could be considered a warrior. Before undertaking his vision quest, Quanah had to seek advice from a puhakut, who explained to him the rituals that he would have to perform to contact the spirit world. The puhakut instructed Quanah to first clean himself in a spring and then travel out into the wilderness to find a suitable place to fast and pray. He could bring with him only a buffalo-hide robe, a pipe, some tobacco, and a flint. After he found an appropriate spot, he was to ask the Great Spirit to reveal to him his guardian spirit. He was then to offer this spirit smoke from his pipe.

Quanah continued his fast for three days without receiving any signs from the spirit world and was by then

A medicine man, or puhakut. *An individual who had demonstrated supernatural power would acquire this title and be highly regarded among tribe members.*

in a hallucinatory state from hunger and exposure. On the fourth day, he noticed an eagle circling above him. As he gazed at it, the bird dove toward the ground and grabbed in its talons a snake that had been lying between two small stones. The bird flew off with its prey, and as it was doing so, lost one of its feathers.

The feather floated down directly toward the young man's feet. As it descended, he heard a voice telling him that his vision quest was completed. Quanah picked up the feather and the two stones between which the snake had hidden itself and placed them in a small rawhide bag—his medicine bundle. Medicine was the power with which a warrior was endowed. Quanah's was very strong because the eagle was a skillful hunter and the snake was the age-old symbol of the Comanche people.

When Quanah returned to his camp, the puhakut told him that he was now known to the Great Spirit as Serpent Eagle but that he must keep the name to himself. He was now a full-fledged member of the Comanche warrior class and was entitled to accompany war parties. These events probably occurred sometime in the late 1850s, a time when the Comanches would need every warrior they could muster.

Texans stave off an Indian attack. As the settlers grew more numerous, so too did the Comanche raids on their homesteads.

4

A SWIFTLY SHRINKING HOMELAND

One of the most significant events in Comanche-U.S. relations occurred in 1855. During the spring of that year, several hundred members of the Penateka band agreed to stop raiding white homesteads and settle on some 20,000 acres of reservation land along the Brazos River in western Texas. (A decade earlier, Texas had become part of the United States.) Before this capitulation, no Comanche band had even considered either settling in one area or giving up rights to even a small portion of the Comanchería. Now, however, the Penatekas ceded hundreds of acres of their homeland and agreed to take up farming, like their non-Indian neighbors.

To Peta Nokona and the other Comanche leaders, such an action was unthinkable. In response, the Detsanayukas and the other Comanches stepped up their raids against Texas settlers, who were becoming even more numerous. This was because the Penatekas' agreement allowed the United States to build a fort at Clear Fork on the Brazos River—the very edge of the Comanchería.

The Comanches' raiding now brought swift retaliation from the U.S. military. Early in 1856, President Franklin Pierce instructed Secretary of War Jefferson Davis to select a corps of officers to command the 2nd Cavalry. These men, as well as their troops, were to be chosen specifically for their horsemanship and their ability to fight mounted adversaries.

After launching their forays, Comanche raiders had previously been safe from attack once they crossed the Red River into the Comanchería. After the 2nd Cavalry came to the region and were later joined by Texas Ranger units, this was no longer true. The troops pursued the Indians back to their camps, indiscriminately slaughtering Comanche men, women, and children. Comanche warriors were no more merciful to white settlers. But death tolls were much higher among the Indians because their camps were home to hundreds of people and the soldiers had superior firepower. This increase in Plains warfare would determine the course of Quanah Parker's life.

In early May of 1858, a force composed of Texas Rangers and Tonkawa warriors set out onto the Plains in search of Comanches, any Comanches. Texas lawmakers were determined either to kill or drive out all of the Indians living within the state's borders. They therefore sent out small units whose only orders were to find and attack Indian camps.

On May 10, Tonkawa scouts discovered, in Detsanayuka territory, a recently vacated butchering site, evidence that the Comanches had just completed a hunt. The Tonkawas knew that the Comanches would head straight back to their camp to finish preparing the meat. Therefore, the Rangers and their scouts set off along the Detsanayukas' trail.

Just before dawn of the next day, they came upon a small group of tipis. This was not the main encampment but a sort of lookout camp that guarded the approach to the rest of the band's tipis. On this occasion, however, the

Texas Rangers about to go on a scouting expedition. Considered brave and resourceful, the Rangers were brutal in their attacks on Comanche villages.

Comanche guards were fast asleep, unaware that the U.S. forces were on their trail.

The Rangers attacked, taking the sleeping guards by surprise. Soldiers rode through tipis and fired at every Indian that they saw. The troops could not afford to allow any of them to escape and warn Peta Nokona and the other warriors of the coming attack. One Detsanayuka guard did manage to get away, but he was hotly pursued by the Rangers and Tonkawas.

When the Texas forces finally reached the entrance to the canyon in which the main Detsanayuka encampment was hidden, they were faced with several hundred wide-awake warriors—hardly what they expected. However, a Tonkawa sharpshooter quickly turned the odds in their favor by killing the great Pohebits Quasho, Quanah's grandfather. His death was very demoralizing to the Detsanayukas because the war leader, who was thought to possess great mystic power, was unable to escape the bullet.

The Tonkawas and Rangers attacked quickly and many Comanche warriors were killed. But after several hours, the battle showed no signs of ending nor did the Comanches show any signs of surrendering. The Rangers had, however, managed to drive the warriors into a side canyon.

Although the Comanches greatly outnumbered the soldiers, the Indians could not compete with the troops' weapons. The tribe had never possessed many guns and certainly none of the newly developed revolvers used by the Texas Rangers. This invention allowed the Rangers to fire six bullets before reloading, an innovation that proved devastating for Peta Nokona and his warriors.

Tonkawa Indians, a tribe that had occupied the southern Plains before the Comanches migrated there. As a way of retaliating against their Comanche enemies, many Tonkawas served the U.S. Army as scouts.

The Detsanayukas held their ground long enough for Quanah and the other young warriors to escape and rejoin the rest of the band. They exited the canyon by one of the many well-hidden side trails and headed for one of their other campsites, where they planned to wait for the survivors. Several hours later, they were joined by Peta Nokona and other warriors who had managed to escape the canyon siege.

In the months that followed, Peta Nokona and his Detsanayuka warriors took their revenge as often and as viciously as they could. They raided dozens of farmsteads, attacked wagon trains, and killed Texans at an alarming rate. Their actions so worried the U.S. government that the secretary of war lifted a restriction that forbade federal troops from crossing into the Comanches' territory.

In the autumn of 1858, Brigadier General David Twiggs set off after the Comanches again. Once more, Peta Nokona and his band were the objects of attack. Twiggs discovered their encampment in the Wichita Mountains, and this time the Comanches did not have any advance warning. At dawn, the troops descended on the sleeping Indians and began firing upon anything that moved. However, they were not particularly well organized in their attack, and most of the Detsanayukas were able to escape, including Peta Nokona and his family. But Twiggs and his men did inflict a cost almost as terrible as death: They burned all of the Indians' dwellings and stores of food and took several hundred of their horses. With winter not far off, the Indians were left with no supplies.

Peta Nokona now realized that his band was not safe anywhere in its traditional homeland. He therefore decided to move his people westward onto the Llano Estacado to a place that was hidden and easily defendable. He chose a site along a fork of the Red River where it

Palo Duro Canyon in about 1899. Colonel Mackenzie had his greatest victory over the Comanches at the canyon in 1874, making the area generally safe for white settlement.

flowed through Palo Duro Canyon in the Texas Panhandle. The site was almost impossible for any non-Comanche to find. Even if anyone were to discover it, there was only a narrow path in and out. It was impossible for a large force of mounted soldiers to fight their way in. The Detsanayukas would survive there as best they could and plan their revenge for the spring.

The band's desire to punish the Texans was heightened in early 1859 during a visit from some of their Kotsoteka relatives. Their leader, Skin of a Bear, brought news that the Penatekas had been forced to leave their reservation after continual threats by the Texas settlers who lived around them. Armed settlers had even entered the reservation and fired on the Indian inhabitants. The Texans had forced the federal government to agree to move the reservation to land in Oklahoma.

Skin of a Bear went on to explain that the Penatekas had been given only a few days' notice of their impending move. They were not allowed to round up their livestock or harvest their fields. In fact, the federal agent for the reservation, Robert Neighbors, had fought long and hard to convince the Texas government to give the Indians more time, but he was given no support in Washington. After Neighbors had overseen the move, he returned to the reservation to take care of personal matters and was murdered by a Texan who did not approve of Neighbors's defense of the Indians. Ironically, Neighbors was killed soon after he had written to his wife that he had "crossed all the Indians out of the heathen land of Texas and [was] now out of the land of the Philistines."

These actions only served to solidify Peta Nokona's conviction that white officials were not to be trusted, a belief he surely passed on to Quanah. When the summer of 1859 arrived, Peta Nokona again began to make devastating raids on the settlements around Waco, Texas. All efforts by the local militia and a U.S. cavalry brigade to put a stop to the Comanche war leader were unsuccessful.

It was not until Texas governor Sam Houston sought help from veteran soldier Lawrence "Sul" Ross that the tide again began to turn. Ross gathered together a group of ex-Rangers and former members of the 2nd Cavalry and went in search of the Detsanayukas. He planned to use the same methods that had worked for Twiggs and earlier regiments—find the Indians' encampment and kill them as they slept.

In the autumn of 1859, Peta Nokona, Quanah, and most of the other Detsanayuka warriors departed for the last buffalo hunt of the season. They left behind a few warriors to defend the camp as Naduah and the other women packed up the belongings in preparation for moving to another campsite farther west. Ross and his raiders came upon this scene and immediately rushed into the canyon, firing at the Comanches.

The Indians scattered, some on horseback and some on foot. Many, however, were rounded up and taken captive.

An engraving of Lawrence "Sul" Ross, who put together a fighting force of veteran soldiers to hunt down the Detsanayuka band. In 1859, Ross and his troops recaptured Quanah's mother and returned her to her Texas relatives.

Among them was Naduah, who was recognized as a white woman despite her many years under the hot Plains sun. She, her infant daughter, and the rest of the captives were taken back to nearby Fort Radziminski. There, she was questioned about her past, but she remembered nothing other than her former name.

On the slim chance that she was indeed Cynthia Ann Parker, fort officials sent for her relatives, who identified her and brought her back to their home in Texas. However, Naduah had no desire to resume a life among whites. The Comanche way of life was the only one that she knew. Her Parker relatives refused to allow her to return to her husband and sons, whom she never saw again. Topsannah was dead within a year of their capture, and Naduah died only three years later, probably from a combination of depression and a non-Indian disease.

When Peta Nokona and the buffalo hunters returned to Palo Duro Canyon, they found that their supplies and dwellings had been destroyed and many of their wives and children had either been killed or taken captive. Once again, the Detsanayukas gathered up the remains of their belongings, buried their dead, and moved to a new campsite. They spent the winter mourning their losses and attempting to carry on their way of life. Peta Nokona would never remarry.

When the spring of 1861 came, the Detsanayukas went out onto the Plains to meet with Comanchero traders and replenish their dwindling supplies. There, Peta Nokona learned that Apaches had been trespassing on what the Comanches considered to be their territory. He immediately began organizing a war party to drive them out.

Leaving Quanah at home to oversee band activities, he set off for the southern border of the Comanchería. Ten days later, the warriors returned victorious. However, Peta Nokona had been gravely wounded and was brought back on a *travois*, a frame attached to two poles and dragged

Cynthia Ann Parker, Quanah's mother, with Topsannah, her daughter. Except for her blue eyes, Cynthia Ann was indistinguishable from other Comanche women.

by a horse. He died soon after, leaving his sons as orphans.

According to Comanche custom, places of death had to be deserted and the possessions of the dead scattered. In Peta Nokona's case, this practice left his sons with nothing. Pecos, too young to live on his own, was sent to live among the Yamparikas. Quanah, on the other hand, was old enough to make his own way but had no wealth of his own among the Detsanayukas. He therefore had to live with another band where he could acquire possessions and a reputation.

Not long after Peta Nokona's death, Quanah left the band that he had known all his life and went to live among the Kotsotekas. At first, he was allowed only to tend the war leader's horses and perform menial tasks for him. But Quanah's skill as a hunter and warrior was soon recognized, and he was allowed to join war parties.

On one occasion, Quanah even saved the Kotsoteka chief from a Mexican bullet. The incident occurred during a Kotsoteka raid on a Mexican village, where the warriors came up against a troop of Mexican soldiers. In the melee, Quanah spied a soldier drawing aim on the Kotseteka chief. Urging his pony forward, the young man managed to sink his spear into the soldier before he could pull the trigger. This heroic act helped increase Quanah's standing within the band.

Although Quanah quickly rose to prominence among the Kotsotekas, he never felt at home with them. In the autumn of 1862, the Quahadi band came to visit their Kotsoteka relatives. The Quahadi chief, Yellow Bear, saw Quanah's potential and invited him to join the band. Quanah accepted and returned with them to the Llano Estacado. In only a few years, he became a hunt leader and a respected warrior.

In 1866, Quanah's position among the Quahadis changed from exalted to hunted. For several months, he had been courting Yellow Bear's daughter, whose name

was Weckeah. However, because he had not yet built up a stock of horses, he could not afford to pay the chief for his daughter. In Comanche society, a man had to exchange horses for his chosen wife in order to make up for her father's loss of her labor. The usual price was 8 to 10 horses, a very large number for a young man to obtain.

Because Quanah could not manage such an expense, Yellow Bear decided to marry Weckeah to another young warrior. This man's father was a powerful war leader and provided his son with more than the required bride price. However, before the transaction could take place, Quanah and Weckeah eloped. They were joined in their flight by 20 young rebel warriors. The group planned to start its own band, make its own raids, and hunt its own buffalo.

For several months, Yellow Bear, the jilted groom, and his father searched for the couple, whose actions were considered criminal in Comanche society. Meanwhile,

Plains Indians used animal-drawn frames, called travois, *to transport their belongings. Quanah's father, Peta Nokona, was brought back to camp on a travois after being seriously wounded in battle.*

Quanah's newly formed band was quickly acquiring a reputation among the inhabitants—Indian and non-Indian alike—of the southern Plains. Before a year had passed, the group had swelled to more than 200 members and had built up a stock of several hundred horses, most of which had been stolen during raids in west Texas.

In the spring of 1867, Yellow Bear finally caught up with the outlaw band at a Comanchero trade fair. The two groups prepared for a battle, but before the fighting could break out, a Quahadi elder suggested that Quanah and Yellow Bear try to reach a settlement without bloodshed. He pointed out that the Comanches could not afford to lose warriors under any circumstances and certainly not at each other's hands. The elder proposed that Quanah should make a payment of horses to both Yellow Bear and the other suitor. The three men agreed. When the bargaining was completed, Weckeah remained Quanah's wife and the members of his breakaway band rejoined the Quahadis.

Throughout the summer and into the fall of 1867, the Quahadis—as well as most of the other Comanche bands—continued to raid Texas settlements and steal Texan livestock. These attacks produced a growing hysteria among the white settlers. By this time, Comanche warriors such as Quanah had earned a fearsome nickname. The settlers called them Red Raiders. This epithet struck terror into the souls of non-Indians, particularly those who had experienced a Comanche raid and had somehow escaped with their life.

With ever-increasing frequency, the Texans petitioned Washington to put a stop to the Comanches by whatever means necessary. In response, the U.S. government would first attempt diplomatic coercion. When this failed, they would resort to a bloody campaign to subdue the Red Raiders.

5

THE LLANO ESTACADO IS CONQUERED

Phillip McCusker, pictured with a Wichita Indian leader. McCusker, who had lived among the Comanches, had heard of Cynthia Ann Parker's return to her Texas relatives. At the 1867 Medicine Lodge council, Mc- Cusker related to Quanah the facts of his mother's unhappy life—and death—among the whites.

In an effort to stem the violence on the Plains, Congress created the Indian Peace Commission in 1867. This group, which consisted of political and military representatives, quickly arranged to meet with the leaders of several Plains tribes in a council at Medicine Lodge Creek in Kansas. Neither the Kotsotekas nor the Quahadis were officially represented at this meeting. However, Quanah did attend—as an observer.

In the summer of 1867, Quanah had been very ill, suffering high fevers and delirium. By summer's end, however, he had recovered and was on his feet, but he was too weak to hunt or raid. Hearing about the upcoming Medicine Lodge council, Quanah became curious to hear what the whites would propose. He decided that he was fit enough to travel and set off for the meeting.

This decision eventually proved to be significant for Quanah in a way he could never have foreseen. Also attending the peace council was a white man named Phillip McCusker who had been living among the Comanches and was married to a Comanche woman. McCuster knew the story of Cynthia Ann Parker—her abduction by the Comanches and her recapture by the whites.

McCusker related to Quanah how his mother and sister had lived unhappily with their white relatives and had died only a few years after the reunion. To commemorate the memory of his mother, Quanah decided to take on her surname, which previously had been unknown to him.

At the Medicine Lodge council, the U.S. representatives warned the tribal leaders that white settlement of their territories was inevitable and that they were well advised to make peace with the United States. The commissioners promised the Indians that they would be compensated for the cession of large portions of their territories. They would be given lands away from white settlement and receive annual payments of goods worth $25,000 for 30 years as well as tools and equipment for constructing "civilized" settlements. In return, the commissioners asked the Indians to cease all attacks against whites and to refrain from interfering with the construction of forts, railroads, and roads through their territory.

A sketch depicting the peace council at Medicine Lodge Creek, Kansas. For Quanah, the meeting was a failure. He left the council saying, "Tell the white chiefs that the Quahadis are warriors, and will surrender only when the blue coats come and whip us."

Although the Indian leaders recognized the force behind the commissioners' words, they reminded the men that the U.S. government was well known for breaking its promises to the Indians. Toshaway, a leader of the Yamparikas, was particularly wary after the fiasco with his band's reservation in Texas and the murder of Robert Neighbors. He told the commissioners, "My young men are a scoff . . . among the other nations. I shall wait till next spring to see if these things will be given us, if they are not, I and my young men will return with our wild brothers to live on the prairie."

Another Yamparika leader, Ten Bears, spoke at length about the Indians' plight, but ultimately it was to no avail. In concluding his speech, he said:

> If the Texans had kept out of my country, there might have been peace. . . . The Texans have taken away the places where the grass grew the thickest and the timber was best. Had we kept that, we might have done the things you ask. But it is too late. The whites have the country which we loved, and we wish only to wander on the prairie until we die.

Still, a treaty was eventually drawn up and signed by many of the Indian leaders, including Toshaway, Ten Bears, and eight other Comanche headmen. Their main reason for doing so was to speed up the usual distribution of goods that followed such meetings with U.S. officials. The Indians clearly had no faith in the words of the white men and merely hoped to get what they could from them while they had the chance. The leaders also knew that the commissioners would not leave until they obtained their signatures. General of the Army William T. Sherman warned the Indians, "You can no more stop this than you can stop the sun or moon; you must submit and do the best you can."

As far as the U.S. government was concerned, the Treaty of Medicine Lodge Creek had settled all of its

Yamparika leader Ten Bears had visited Washington, D.C., and noted that "important" men wore spectacles. He thus bought a pair and acquired the habit of wearing them when dealing with whites.

problems with the Comanche tribe. However, the commissioners made the same mistake that their Spanish predecessors had made. They viewed the Comanche political structure in terms of their own. The U.S. Constitution permits Congress and the president to make decisions that are binding on all U.S. citizens. In Comanche culture, there was no such supreme lawmaking body. The Kotsotekas and the Quahadis had not been represented at Medicine Lodge Creek. Therefore, these bands felt that they were in no way bound by the terms of the treaty.

Toshaway, one of the prominent Comanches who spoke for his people at the Medicine Lodge council in 1867.

Quanah left the council indignant, swearing never to give up. In the months that followed, he and the Quahadis stepped up their attacks on settlers. The treaty's ratification was delayed for quite some time, during which the Indian signatory waited in vain for their promised lands and goods to be provided. When nothing was forthcoming, the warriors naturally took to raiding again, particularly in Texas. Because of the history of Texas, many Plains Indians viewed it as an entity separate from the United States and, consequently, saw no reason to believe that the treaty restrictions applied there.

When the borders of the reservation were finally formalized and agencies built on them, many Indians relocated to them, including some members of the Kotsoteka band. But they found that the promised supplies were either not available or pitifully minimal. Some stayed only for the winter and moved back to the Plains when the buffalo returned.

A Kotsoteka leader expressed his opinion of the reservation system to an agent who tried to convince him to remain. He said that "there [was] no reason for a Comanche to come back to the reservation until Comanches on the reservations live better than Comanches on the prairie." Others pretended to settle down to a sedentary life while continuing to send raiding parties into Texas.

The Quahadis steered altogether clear of issues pertaining to reservations and treaties with the U.S. government. As a result, they were blamed for almost all of the depredations that occurred in the late 1860s. Reservation agents did not want their bosses in Washington to think them incompetent or unable to control their Indian charges, so they found it convenient to point to the Quahadis when reservation Indians conducted raids.

One of these clandestine raids in 1871 forced the U.S. government to begin an all-out hunt for Quanah and the Quahadis. In mid-May, a party of approximately 150 reservation Kiowa and Comanche warriors attacked a wagon train and tortured and murdered the teamsters who drove it. One driver escaped and made his way to nearby Fort Richardson, where Philip Sheridan, the general of the army, was staying.

Sheridan immediately ordered that the attackers be captured. He called on Colonel Ranald Mackenzie, a fellow Civil War veteran, to see to the matter. Mackenzie traced the guilty warriors to the Fort Sill reservation and

confronted the Indian agent, Lawrie Tatum. Tatum had
previously come under fire for his inability to control the
Indians who were in his charge. He admitted that the
warriors were from among those in his jurisdiction and
subsequently turned them over.

However, to shift blame away from himself and the
failed reservation policies of the federal government,
Tatum complained at great length to General Sheridan
that as long as the Quahadis were able to continue their
traditional way of life, the other Indians would be
unsatisfied with reservation life. He was in part correct,
but it is doubtful that the Comanches could ever have
become "satisfied" with reservation life.

Tatum proposed that a military body be formed to
apprehend and either bring in or kill off the Quahadis.
This was easier said than done, however. The Quahadis
were safely entrenched in their remote homeland, the

*The number of horses that a
Comanche warrior possessed
was one of the major ways to
measure his wealth and status
within the tribe. Comanches
on the southern Plains continually raided Texan and
Mexican farms to steal horses.*

Llano Estacado. Few but the Comanches had a grasp of its geography.

Sheridan must have realized that in order to stop the Quahadis he would have to authorize a costly, bloody, and probably lengthy war against them. Although the decision was difficult, it did not take Sheridan long to reach it. He authorized the funds and men needed and placed them under the command of Colonel Mackenzie. Mackenzie's task was then to turn the soldiers into mounted Plains fighters. The training took up most of the late spring and summer of 1871.

By August, the troops were ready to make their first foray into Quahadi territory. They set off from Fort Richardson and headed west. For the next six weeks, the regiment encountered many signs of Quanah and his band but were unable to locate their camp because the Indians had retreated far into the Llano Estacado. Mackenzie was forced to give up on this first attempt, and he returned with his men to the fort.

The colonel's next effort was a little more successful. He was able to find the Comanches with the aid of his Tonkawa scouts, but he probably regretted this breakthrough by the time the escapade was over. This mission was the previously described mishap on the Llano Estacado during which Mackenzie lost several men and more than 70 horses to Quanah and his small group of warriors.

Mackenzie and other military leaders in the region spent the winter of 1871–72 devising a plan of attack for the following summer. When it was launched, Mackenzie and his 4th Cavalry headed out onto the Llano Estacado again, but this time they had a guide. Mackenzie had hired a Mexican who had made many trading expeditions into Quahadi territory. However, even with his guide, Mackenzie was unable to inflict any damage on the band.

Some members of the U.S. Army's 10th Cavalry, an all-black unit. These "buffalo soldiers," as they were called by the Indians, played a major role in opening the foreboding Llano Estacado to non-Indians.

Quanah and the other leaders had apparently decided it best not to engage the soldiers directly and instead led them on an uneventful chase through the Llano Estacado. Eventually, as the Quahadis had probably intended, Mackenzie was forced to return his weary and demoralized troops to the fort.

Although this third attempt was unsuccessful, it was not entirely fruitless. Mackenzie now had a basic knowledge of the geography of the Llano Estacado. No longer would he have to worry about becoming lost or misdirected there. Despite the negative criticism he was receiving in the Texas newspapers, Mackenzie was steadily accumulating the experience that he would need to defeat the Comanche raiders.

During the 4th Cavalry's next expedition, their research paid off. In early autumn of 1872, Mackenzie and his men discovered a Kotsoteka encampment. He gave the order to attack, and the soldiers charged into the cluster of tipis. The surprised Indians were overwhelmed and quickly defeated. When the battle ended, dozens of tipis were destroyed and at least 50 warriors lay dead. The soldiers rode away with more than 100 Kotsoteka women and many hundreds of horses.

The soldiers made camp some distance from the Kotsotekas' ruined camp and rejoiced in their victory. However, unknown to them, a Kotsoteka warrior had escaped the slaughter and raced to the Quahadi encampment only a few miles away. He informed Quanah and the other leaders of the incident and told them where they could find Mackenzie. The Quahadi leaders quickly

Quanah in war dress. Throughout the first half of the 1870s, the Quahadis and their cunning leader were able to foil the many attempts by the U.S. Army to subdue them.

organized a war party and set off. Without losing a single warrior, Quanah and his party harried the soldiers and recaptured the stolen horses; however, they were unable to free the women. Again Mackenzie was forced to return to Fort Richardson without Quanah Parker, but he had at least done some harm to the Comanches.

During the remainder of 1872 and throughout 1873, the cavalry and the Comanches traded blows, but neither could achieve a decisive victory over the other. However, the army's continued practice of burning the Indians' property and stores of meat began to take its toll. These losses were made worse by the dwindling buffalo herds, which were being steadily killed off by non-Indian hunters.

When the spring of 1874 arrived, the remaining Quahadis and Kotsotekas were in a desperate situation. A Quahadi named Eschiti proposed that the Indians should direct their attacks on the buffalo hunters. Eschiti was a powerful puhakut and war leader who had insisted for a long time that the Indians could bring back the buffalo and get rid of the white encroachers if they observed certain rituals and trusted in his powers. The band eventually decided to try his suggestions.

Eschiti professed to have the ability to make his people bulletproof and therefore invincible. "Those white men can't shoot you," he promised. "With my medicine I will stop all their guns. . . . You will wipe them all out." Quanah and the other Quahadi leaders agreed to follow him and organized a war party, which was joined by several Kiowa and Cheyenne warriors from the Fort Sill reservation. They selected a trading post at Adobe Walls as the first stop in their upcoming defeat of the whites. This place had special significance to the Comanches because in 1864 it had been the site of an attack on the tribe by the renowned soldier Kit Carson.

To surprise the hunters the Indians planned to attack at sunrise. Unfortunately for them, most of the men at the trading post were already awake repairing a roof beam that had collapsed during the night. Therefore, when the Indians began their assault, they were met with fire from the traders' powerful buffalo-hunting guns.

The attack lasted several hours without any significant results. Quanah and the other warriors decided to end their assault when "prophet" Eschiti's horse was shot out from under him. Eschiti blamed the failure of his "medicine" on some members of the war party who had violated a taboo by killing a skunk.

After this crushing failure, the Quahadis found themselves under attack from all sides. Quanah and his people again sought the remote safety of the Palo Duro Canyon, but it again served as the setting for tragedy. In late November, Mackenzie and his 4th Cavalry found and attacked the Indians. Although most of them escaped, they did so on foot and without any of their food, belongings, or shelters. Mackenzie then ordered his men to shoot the Quahadis' more than 1,000 horses because he knew that there was no other way to prevent the

Adobe Walls, 1874, a depiction by artist John Eliot Jenkins. Here, Quanah's warriors made their final major assault on the buffalo hunters who were destroying their way of life. The unsuccessful attack foreshadowed the Quahadis' upcoming surrender.

Indians from retaking them.

The Quahadis were able to survive by hunting small game and gathering roots and other plant foods as they made the long trek southward to Mexico. Quanah and the other warriors realized that they needed to get out of Texas for awhile and decided it was best to head for a warmer place. This decision proved to be a good one because in less than a year, the band had rebuilt its herds to almost 2,000 horses by stealing from Mexican ranches. Quanah believed that the band would be well prepared by the spring of 1875 to return to Palo Duro for the annual buffalo hunt.

However, this was not to be. Out of the north came three Comanches—who had surrendered to the U.S. government—accompanied by a reservation employee named J. J. Sturm. They had been sent by Colonel Mackenzie to talk the Quahadis into surrendering to the reservation forces. The three Comanches, one of whom was Quahadi, stressed to their friends and relatives that the Plains were no longer safe. They told the band that they would surely die if they tried to return to their traditional way of life.

The Quahadi leaders had a long night of intense debate over their options. None of them wished to give up their unrestricted lives on the Plains, and they knew that reservation life was not desirable. However, in the end, they realized that the prospect of more death and destruction at the hands of the U.S. military was beyond their people's endurance. At the very least, the reservation offered them survival.

The next morning, the Quahadi leaders gave the messengers their answer. A few days later, Quanah and several other warriors left for Fort Sill to surrender. The last of the Comanches would soon be gone from the southern Plains.

A watercolor of Fort Sill,
in present-day Oklahoma.
Quanah and his band sur-
rendered at this post in 1875.

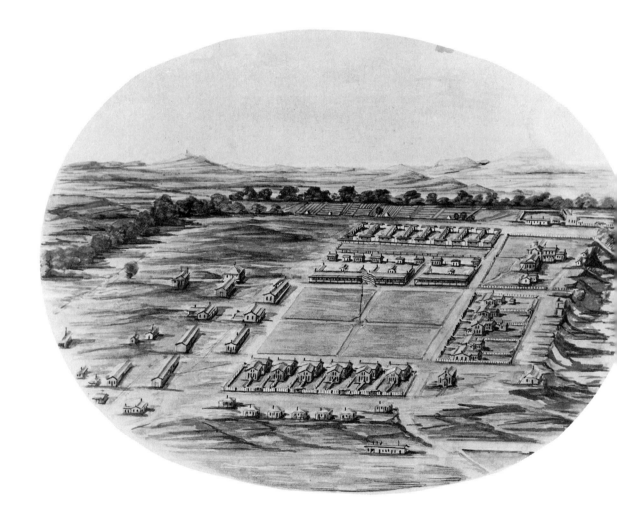

6

AMONG THE
AMERICANS

On a bright afternoon in late May of 1875, a crowd gathered at the entrance gate of Fort Sill in Indian Territory. Messages had been steadily coming in with the news that a group of Quahadi Comanches were heading toward the stockade. However, it was curiosity, rather than fear, that brought the people out. Most of them were members of other Comanche bands or Kiowa and Kiowa-Apache Indians who were living on the reservation. They were patiently waiting for the imminent meeting between U.S. Army colonel Ranald Mackenzie and the warrior who had outwitted him for more than four years—Quanah Parker.

It had taken several weeks and many messenger parties passing back and forth between the Quahadi leaders and Mackenzie before the band actually arrived at Fort Sill. This moment had long been imagined by both the Indian and non-Indian inhabitants of west Texas. For the reservation Comanches, it signaled an end to the tribe's ancient way of life, of which the Quahadis were the last symbol. For the settlers of west Texas, the surrender meant a probable end to the bloody and destructive raids that had plagued them for the last 40 years.

Both groups eagerly waited to lay eyes on the man who, with a mere 400 warriors, had eluded, taunted, and embarassed Mackenzie and his forces, which numbered more than 3,000. Many expected a violent confrontation. However, according to people who witnessed the meeting, both men were cordial and respectful of each other's bravery and determination in their past encounters.

Quanah was proud of the way he had led his people away from war. He had brought them onto the reservation without soldiers guarding them. Later, in an interview, he described the event and one of his final battles with Mackenzie before surrendering.

> I came into Fort Sill, no ride me in like horse or lead me by halter like cow. . . . I fought . . . Mackenzie. He brave man, good soldier, but uses two thousand men; many wagons, horses and mules. Me, I only had 450 braves, no supply train, ammunition and guns like him. I used this knife. . . . Mackenzie no catch me.

In early June the Comanches' traditional way of life officially came to an end. The Quahadi band turned over its vast herd of horses, surrendered its weapons, and set up its tipis on the reservation grounds.

Soon after Quanah arrived at the fort, he made Mackenzie aware that his mother had been a Texan. He did so mainly in the hope that his opinions and suggestions might carry some weight when the colonel decided the fate of the Quahadis. But he also had another motive: Everyone who spoke with Quanah about his childhood and adolescence attested that he was wholeheartedly devoted to his mother's memory. With Mackenzie's help, Quanah was able to acquire a portrait of his mother and sister painted shortly before the child's death.

During the next few years, Quanah and the Quahadis did their best to survive the difficult transition to reservation life. However, even their best attempts

Quanah, in a posed photograph taken on the reservation. He was proud to have led his warriors into the fort unaccompanied by any military guard.

brought only the barest minimum of comforts. The Indians' efforts to adapt were constantly impeded by the U.S. government, which often failed to provide desperately needed supplies of food, clothing, and utensils. The ineffectual management of the Fort Sill Indian Agency also contributed to the problems Indians faced living on the reservation. James M. Haworth, the reservation agent, was continually bombarded with conflicting instructions as to his duties and the government's objectives for Indian acculturation.

Because of the food shortages, many warriors continued to venture out onto the Plains in search of buffalo. Although many Indian agents cast a blind eye to this practice, the Indians were technically forbidden to leave the reservation grounds. And the cavalry was kept busy trying to bring the hunting parties back. This problem afforded Quanah and several other prominent Comanches a chance to gain favor with the reservation officials by going out in search of the escapees and convincing them to return to Fort Sill. Quanah was particularly adept at this. Once, he brought back a large group of escapees and, because he was highly regarded by the officials, convinced the military men to refrain from punishing the Indians too severely.

The ration problem continued unabated between 1875 and 1877 and resulted in increasing unrest among the Indians. The situation was made worse when the U.S. government decided to have the functions of the Fort Sill agency handled by the Wichita Agency, which was located in Anadarko, Oklahoma, some 30 miles to the north. The move was opposed by the Comanches, Kiowas, and Kiowa-Apaches because it would require them to travel even farther for their rations. The army was also against the move, complaining that they would be unable to keep a careful watch on the Indians from that distance.

Reservation Comanches receiving goods from U.S. officials. Poor management at Fort Sill often resulted in the Indians' not getting the supplies they were promised.

Caught in the middle, Haworth decided to resign and leave the problem to his successor.

This man was P. B. Hunt, a former Internal Revenue Service worker from Kentucky, who took over the post of Indian agent at Anadarko in the spring of 1878. Hunt was a bit more realistic about the Indians' prospects for survival on the reservation. He promptly began petitioning Washington to change its emphasis from farming to ranching because the reservation's environment was more suited to it. Earlier, Hunt's predecessor had written to Washington officials about the reservation's "fine nutritious grass in inexhaustible quantities, good and plenty of water, and good shelter."

As a result of Hunt's efforts, in 1879 the federal government provided him with funds to purchase more than 500 head of cattle. The Indians were slightly successful at ranching, so Hunt requested that all of their treaty funds be spent on cattle in order to help them increase their herds. His petition was denied, but Congress did appropriate $30,000 for buying cattle. One of the more successful ranchers among the Comanches was Quanah Parker. By 1884, his herd had grown so large that he was able to sell several dozen heads to the Indian agency for distribution among his people.

Despite the Comanches' limited successes with ranching, they and the other Fort Sill Indians continued to suffer throughout the 1880s from inadequate rations. Congress, tired of the continual pleas for funds by reservation agents, rarely provided enough money to buy the needed supplies. In the comfort of their offices in the East, congressmen did not bother to acknowledge the federal government's responsibility for the deplorable conditions on the reservation. Instead, they preferred to blame the Indians themselves. As one congressman noted, "the Indians will never do a thing for their self-support so long as we concede to them every single thing which their distended stomachs demand."

In order to overcome these obstacles, Hunt devised a scheme that would come to greatly affect the Comanches' political structure and help bring Quanah to its forefront. Almost since the reservation's inception, Texas cattlemen had been illegally driving their stock onto the Indians' rich pasture lands. The federal government could do little to stop this. It could afford neither the supplies to fence in the land nor the men to patrol it.

Hunt realized that he had to come up with a plan that took into account the wants of the ranchers and the needs of the Indians. Because the Indians were making little use of their pasture land, Hunt decided that it would be to their best advantage to lease the land to the ranchers. However, Hunt needed approval to implement his idea.

P. B. Hunt, standing at left. As agent of the Wichita Agency, Hunt changed the reservation's emphasis from farming to ranching. Quanah became quite successful as a rancher and also benefited greatly from his alliance with the Texas cattlemen.

First of all, he needed the permission of the Indians themselves. Second, he needed the go-ahead from Washington. He soon found that neither was forthcoming. The Indians immediately divided themselves into pro- and antileasing factions. The former was composed mainly of Comanches (who lived closest to the Texans), and the latter consisted of Kiowas and Kiowa-Apaches (who inhabited the northern portion of the reservation). As for Washington's approval, Hunt was promised the customary "investigation," which meant that nothing would be done in the near future.

Realizing that the debate might go on for quite a while, Hunt began to charge the ranchers to use the pasture

anyway. At the same time, the cattlemen began a campaign to acquire approval from the Indians by putting several of their leaders, including Quanah, Eschiti, and Permansu on their payroll. For his cooperation, Quanah was provided with several hundred cattle and a monthly "salary" of $50.

One of Quanah's first actions in his new position was to lead a proleasing delegation, funded by the cattle companies, to Washington in the spring of 1884. How-

Several practitioners of the peyote religion. Quanah, seated second from left, was able to persuade the federal government to condone peyotism, which was frowned upon by most non-Indians.

ever, all the men got was a promise that the Bureau of Indian Affairs (BIA) office would look into the matter. (The BIA is the agency of the federal government in charge of handling matters concerning Indians.)

In early 1885, the group again traveled to the capital to push for approval of the leasing program. This time, they were able to get a more ready response from the U.S. officials. Both the secretary of the interior and the attorney general refused to legalize the scheme, but neither did they forbid it. Instead, the officials agreed not to intercede while Hunt implemented his plan. Thus, in mid-1885 Quanah and the other Comanches began to receive their "grass payments," which totaled some $20 a year per person.

It is hardly likely that Quanah would have risen so quickly to such a position of power and influence had he still lived freely on the Plains. As a man of only about 40 at this time, he would not yet have been able to achieve the exalted status of band leader, as Peta Nokona had done in his later years. Quanah had surely distinguished himself as a warrior and raider, but in traditional Comanche society these skills were not enough to raise one to the position of headman. Years of experience were also needed to hold such weight among the other band members.

On the reservation, however, several factors worked in Quanah's favor. The most important was the BIA's deliberate undermining of the Comanches' traditional culture. This effort was part of the federal government's plan to compel the Plains Indians to adopt the ways of white Americans. There would no longer be any raiding or warfare on the Plains, officials reasoned, if individual Indian families were tied to fields and livestock.

For the Anadarko agents, the first step in the assimilation process was to replace the old Comanche leaders with new ones who were willing to cooperate with non-Indian officials. Quanah was singled out almost immediately because of his white ancestry and his obvious talents as a leader. Indeed, Ranald Mackenzie was one of his most ardent supporters. Hunt rapidly became one as well. The goodwill of these men, coupled with that of the cattlemen, allowed Quanah to rise rapidly in the Comanche political system.

Meanwhile, the federal government was launching another part of its assimilation plan. The policymakers in Washington realized that the best way to eradicate the Comanches' culture was through their children. If they could be removed from the "bad" influence of their parents and taught mainstream American values, then the difficulties posed by unassimilated Indians could be eliminated in a single generation.

Therefore, several schools were opened on the reservation, and parents were cajoled and threatened into sending their children to them. The agents were even instructed to withhold food from any family whose children did not attend school. Even so, few of these institutions were ever filled to more than half their capacity. The low attendance was no great loss as the schools were rarely provided with enough funds to care for the children who did attend.

Perhaps in response to these threats to their culture, more and more Comanches, including Quanah Parker, were taking to a religious practice whose focus was the consumption of peyote. The Comanches had learned about this narcotic cactus fruit from the Apaches. Peyote induced hallucinations and brought a feeling of tranquility, something the Indians had lost since they had moved to the reservation. Moreover, because peyote rituals had to be performed in groups, they provided a way for scattered families to get together. During the ceremonies, individuals would ingest the drug and then recite sacred songs and prayers, often for many hours at a time.

During Agent Hunt's tenure among the Comanches, there was no official response to peyotism. However, in 1885, Hunt resigned and was replaced by J. Lee Hall, who attempted to ban the practice. This threat afforded Quanah with another opportunity to wield his influence. He was able to bargain with the federal government to allow peyotism by agreeing to send his children to the agency school. Agent Hall quickly came to realize that he would be much better off if he kept himself on Quanah's good side, so he gave up his fight against peyote consumption.

Peyote pins, which are worn by practitioners of peyotism. Today, peyote is used as a sacrament by members of the Native American Church.

By the late 1880s, Quanah and the other Fort Sill leaders had reached an understanding with U.S. officials. The Indians were by no means prospering, but they were beginning to adapt to reservation life. However, in 1887, Congress approved a body of legislation that would throw a monkey wrench into the already uneasy works. Its name was the General Allotment Act (also known as the Dawes Act). This law was formulated largely in response to the increasingly vocal demands for land made by non-Indians. The United States was growing rapidly as the 20th century approached, and the Indians were viewed only as an obstacle to that expansion. One government official described the reservation system as a "bar to the Indians' progress, and our country's development."

Sponsored by Massachusetts senator Henry L. Dawes, the General Allotment Act consisted of two parts. The first focused on reservation land, of which Congress thought that the Indians had too much. Dawes and his committee members proposed that reservations be broken up into 160-acre farmsteads (called allotments) that would then be allotted to heads of individual Indian families. He also made provisions for unmarried people over 18, for orphans, and for individual children, all of whom would receive plots substantially smaller than 160 acres. In areas where land was unsuitable for farming, the allotments would be doubled so livestock could be kept. Land that was left over after the allotments had been assigned was to be sold to non-Indians for settlement, and the funds would be held in trust for the Indians.

The second part of Dawes's proposal dealt with the subject of the Indians' citizenship. The act stated that after the Indians had been provided with their allotments, they would be given full status as U.S. citizens. However, they would be exempted from taxation for 25 years so that they would have time to establish themselves. During that time, the United States would hold their property and funds "in trust," which in effect meant that the Indians would have no more control over their allotted land than they had had over their reservation land.

The Comanches immediately protested the proposed plan, as did virtually every other Indian group that would be affected by it. However, there was little that most of these tribes could do to avoid it. Fortunately for the Comanches, they had Quanah Parker, who in turn had strong ties to the ranching industry. The ranchers were well aware of the implications of allotment on their pasture-leasing operations. With the land open to settlement, the cattlemen would lose most of the cheap grazing land they now had.

Quanah was therefore able to enlist their support to lobby for a delay in the allotment process. As a result, the Fort Sill Indians were able to fend off—for a few years—the Dawes commissioners who would come to force them to accept allotments. Ultimately, though, these Indians would be forced to cave in to the wishes of the non-Indians who surrounded them.

7

PLAYING THE GAME

In the late 1880s, Quanah had a serious brush with death while visiting Fort Worth, Texas, with Yellow Bear (the father of his first wife, Weckeah). After a tiring night out, the two men returned to the hotel. Yellow Bear retired first, extinguishing the gaslight. Quanah later relit it to prepare himself for bed. However, when he turned it off, he did not shut the gas valve enough.

Gas leaked out while they were sleeping. As Quanah related later, he awoke during the night with a "horrible constriction throughout the air passages, pain in the chest, extending down the arms to the elbow." He tried to rouse Yellow Bear but he fainted. Early the next morning a maid entered the room and found Yellow Bear dead. Quanah was alive, but unconscious and seriously ill. After seeing a doctor, the distraught leader hurried back to the reservation.

Despite this nerve-wracking experience, Quanah continued his rise to the top of Comanche politics, and by 1890 his power on the reservation was indisputable. In the early part of that year, he again headed the proleasing faction among the reservation Indians. The previous leasing contracts were about to expire, and Quanah wanted to renew them for another eight years. The antileasing faction wanted a much shorter contract, but Quanah was able to convince them to approve a six-year term.

Quanah was able to adapt to many American ways. He was mystified, however, when he invited his many non-Indian friends to a feast of cooked dog and none of them came.

However, the leasing program was soon threatened from forces outside the reservation. The federal government began to realize that leasing was partly to blame for its difficulties in implementing the General Allotment Act. As a result, in late March, the government instructed its Indian agents to drive all non-Indian cattle from the reservation. The Indians, the cattlemen, and the agents all promised to comply with the directive, but they actually did nothing in this regard. And once again, the federal government did not have the funds or the personnel to follow up on its policies.

In late 1891, the Indians received their first documented approval of leasing, due mainly to the efforts of another proleasing delegation headed by Quanah Parker. The 1-year leases covered some 2 million acres. Soon after they were approved, the federal government instructed Anadarko agent George Day to distribute the grass payments as well as the money that had been held over from previous leases. This money should have been paid to members of the antileasing faction, who had previously refused to accept the funds because of their opposition to leasing.

Instead, Agent Day decided it was better to spend the money on building supplies and wagons. He also hired carpenters to construct houses for the Indians as part of the assimilation policy. Quanah, however, managed to get one of the finest homes on the reservation by asking for funds from his rancher friends. They provided him with $2,000 with which he erected a large, 2-story home with a front porch on both the first and second floors. As a finishing touch, he had several white stars painted on the roof.

Although he had adopted many non-Indian customs, Quanah Parker was fiercely proud of his status among the Comanches and had retained many of his people's

Quanah's Star House at the Fort Sill reservation. Quanah had the stars painted on his roof so that when any army generals visited him they would see that he had more stars than they did.

customs. One was his insistence on wearing his hair in the traditional style, which consisted of two long braids that were tied with fur. He wore braids even when he dressed in American-style suits and hats. One newspaper reporter, describing Quanah in the late 19th century, wrote: "The Chief wears a . . . suit of black broadcloth, neatly fitting his straight body. His shoes are the regular dude style. . . . A gold watch, with chain and charm, dangles from his close-fitting vest. . . . The only peculiar item of his appearance is his long black hair, which he wears in two plaits down his back."

Another tradition that Quanah continued was polygamy, the practice of having more than one wife—he had five. On several occasions Quanah's polygamous ways came under attack from non-Indians, who considerd the practice a pagan custom. During one of his visits to Washington, he met one official who requested that he give up all but one of his wives. The man advised him to go home, choose one wife, and order the others out. Quanah responded, "*You* tell 'em which one I keep." At that point, the official chose to drop the matter.

On another occasion, the wife of one of the reservation agents described to him the religion of his mother's parents. She aroused Quanah's interest so much that he asked how he might take the same religion. She answered that the first thing for him to do would be to give up all but one of his five wives. "In that case," Quanah said, "I keep my religion."

Despite pressure from non-Indians to give up his polygamous ways, Quanah kept his five wives. He is seen here with three of them.

In the early 1890s, the commissioner of Indian affairs (the official who headed the BIA) was T. J. Morgan, who was an extremely devout and traditional Christian and could not tolerate polygamy. He ordered the Anadarko agent to remove Quanah Parker from his seat on the Indians' legal body, the Court of Indian Offenses, which had been created in 1886 to settle disputes between reservation Indians. The agent tried to talk the commissioner out of his decision because he needed Quanah to maintain order at the reservation. The commissioner would not relent, and Quanah was removed.

As a judge on the Court of Indian Offenses, Quanah had dispensed a type of justice that non-Indians could hardly have done to the Indians' satisfaction. This "case" was recounted by Eagle Tail Feather, chief of the Indian police. It involved a dispute between two Comanches, one of whom was contesting the other's right to a certain piece of land.

> Quanah Parker decided the case on old lines. He called in two well-known warriors to decide on the war records of the two men. . . . This man who had the land [asked one of the warriors] "Who is the better man, I or this other fellow?" He thought the warrior would give him credit.
> "All right," the warrior answered him, "you asked me. . . . This other fellow is the better man. I was in a battle where I saw him get off his horse and help a dismounted comrade out of the midst of the enemy. He is a brave man and did a great deed. You had better look out or he will whip you or kill you!"

According to Eagle Tail Feather, it was then up to the man who held the land to come up with "a true account of a braver deed or else give up the land and abide by the decision." He could not do so, and Quanah decided for the complainant. The decision was sound Comanche reasoning, and based upon a war leader's point of view, it was just.

Being a judge on the Court of Indian Offenses had helped Quanah maintain his authority on the reservation. But losing his seat did not perceptibly diminish his prominence. Soon, he again had to contend with the threat of allotment. Lobbyists were beginning to renew pressure on Congress to force the Dawes Act on all Indian Territory reservations. The situation came to a head in 1892, when the federal government sent out a commission, led by David H. Jerome, to bargain with the Indians of the Fort Sill reservation.

Jerome and his men immediately set about to collect the signatures of three-fourths of the reservation's inhabitants, which were needed in order for an agreement to be approved. They coerced the Indians into signing by telling them that they would receive less land if they hesitated. The commission also used biased interpreters who probably did not accurately represent the terms of the proposed agreement.

Eventually, the commission gained the required number of signatures and headed back to Washington. However, the necessary paperwork was put on hold and would not be addressed until 1900. The delay in the official approval of the Jerome Agreement, meant little to the non-Indian settlers in the area. They proceeded to move onto reservation land by the thousands.

In response, Quanah and several other leaders made three trips to Washington in the hope of overturning or at least delaying allotment. During their last trip, Quanah and 3 Kiowa leaders succeeded in retaining an additional 480,000 acres of communal land, which the Indians could continue to lease to the Texas cattlemen.

Throughout the 1890s, Quanah Parker lived well and prospered. He generally cooperated with the non-Indian authorities but avoided total acceptance of the white customs thrust upon him by government agents. He also

Indian police at Anadarko in 1894. These "officers" were responsible for keeping the peace among the reservation Indians.

sought to retain for his people as much independence as possible. When army recruiters tried to enlist Comanches for an all-Indian regiment, Quanah kept his young men from joining. He defended this action by pointing out to the recruiters that missionaries were constantly preaching to his people that war was wrong. He added that the Comanches had accepted reservation life because they were tired of war.

In 1899, a new agent, Colonel James F. Randlett, was appointed to the Fort Sill reservation. He began efforts to have Quanah reinstated to the Court of Indian Offenses. Randlett knew that Quanah would be important to operations at the agency and so he persuaded the commissioner of Indian affairs to grant him the title principal chief of the Comanches. This done, Randlett prepared for the difficulties presented by the impending Jerome Agreement approval.

In June of 1900, Quanah Parker again traveled with a delegation to Washington, but this time it was to receive rather than to present information. Randlett had earlier informed the Indians of the approval of the Jerome Agreement, but many did not believe him. Therefore, he sent the Indian delegation to hear the news directly from its source. Quanah, understanding the inevitability of the U.S. government's actions, accepted the terms while probably planning his next move. Several of the other delegates decided to take legal action. They hired an attorney, incurred many expenses, and spent a year trying

An 1892 photograph of some of Quanah's children. Front row: Len and Baldwin. Back row: Wanada, Weyote, and Harold.

to bargain for better terms, but all to no avail. Ultimately, they were forced to accept defeat, a fate that Quanah Parker had never doubted.

In July 1901, the Comanche, Kiowa, and Kiowa-Apache reservation was opened to non-Indian settlement. But, instead of simply eliminating its borders, as the government had done at other reservations, the commissioner of Indian affairs implemented a lottery system. Agent Randlett requested this procedure because he feared that many of the Indians' allotments would be overrun and usurped if the usual practice took place. The commissioner assigned lottery numbers to approximately 13,000 homesteads, which were to be handed out according to the order in which they were chosen.

During the years after allotment, the Indians' way of life steadily deteriorated. Many of them turned to gambling and alcohol in the towns that sprang up on what had once been Comanche land. Others continued to scrape a meager living out of government supplies and grass payments. Quanah did not sink into the depths of poverty, but he did suffer serious setbacks in his income. He no longer held acreage to lease to cattle ranchers, nor did he receive funds from them for lobbying on their behalf.

However, Quanah did continue his fruitful relationship with Agent Randlett. In the early 1900s, the agent appointed Quanah to the Comanche, Kiowa, and Kiowa-Apache Business Council, which was established as the tribes' governing body. In 1904, Quanah was also able, through Agent Randlett, to secure positions for himself and his daughter Wanada at the agency—he as an assistant farmer and she as an employee of the Indian school.

Quanah was greatly honored when he was asked to represent the American Indian peoples at the inauguration of President Theodore Roosevelt in 1905. The former

Comanche warrior rode with five other Indian representatives in the presidential parade down Constitution
Avenue in Washington, D.C. Roosevelt and Quanah met
again several weeks later when the president visited
Oklahoma Territory on a hunting trip. Quanah told him
of the difficulties that allotment had caused his people.
Roosevelt promised to look into the matter. This time,
the often-used phrase proved to be true.

In 1906, lobbyists from Oklahoma Territory and Texas
began to clamor for the opening of the Indians' 480,000-
acre tract of communal land. Once again, political figures
tried to gain recognition for themselves at the expense of
the Indians. The land in question was bordered by several
towns to which allotment would bring a great deal of
business. Again, Quanah and the Kiowa and Kiowa-
Apache leaders protested, but once again their complaints
fell on deaf ears. Agent Randlett tried to come up with
a plan that had some semblance of justice. He proposed
that the land be allotted to Indian children who had been
born since 1887 and that the remainder be leased.
Congress, however, sought its own course.

A bill was drawn up that provided for the sale of the
tract at the incredibly low price of $1.50 an acre. It was
rushed through the House of Representatives and the
Senate. No congressmen came to the defense of the
Indians. However, it was then that Quanah's abilities as
a spokesman for his people came to fruition. When the
bill was put before President Roosevelt, he threatened to
veto it unless Congress rewrote the legislation to reflect
Agent Randlett's plan. Congress had to comply.

The passage of this legislation marked the loss of the
last communal property held by the Comanches. In the
years that followed, the Indians continued to live as they
had, depending on the government for virtually all of
their needs. As the bans on selling their property were

Depot and general office of the Quanah, Acme, and Pacific Railroad in the town of Quanah, Texas. Quanah was invited to speak at the opening of the town in 1910. He told his audience, "May the Great Spirit always smile on your new town."

lifted, many did not even maintain their own allotments. Most Comanches leased their farms to non-Indians and kept a small plot for themselves.

Quanah Parker would retain his title of principal chief of the Comanches for the remainder of his life, but the title did not mean very much. Most of his duties consisted of serving as a consultant for the agents at Anadarko, lending his voice to business council discussions, and appearing in fairs and celebrations in the area. He even presided over a fair held in his honor, which took place in 1908 and was called the Quanah Parker Celebration.

In 1910, Quanah took part in the opening of a Texas town and a rail line, both named in his honor. In his inaugural speech to the townspeople he said, "May the Great Spirit always smile on your new town." The town of Quanah, which is still in existence today, served at that time as the westernmost stop on the Quanah, Acme, and Pacific Railroad. Quanah invested $40,000 in the railroad company and enjoyed visiting its rail yards to admire the locomotives. He would caress parts of the machines, saying, "My engine; my railroad."

One of the most memorable events that Quanah Parker witnessed was the dedication of a national wildlife refuge on what had once been Comanche land. A significant moment for the once great hunter was the release of a small herd of buffalo onto park land. Although the herd consisted of only 15 animals, it must have been a great joy for him to see their return to the southern Plains.

Quanah's final victory, which occurred shortly before his death, was the symbolic reclaiming of his mother. Cynthia Ann Parker had been buried among her relatives in Texas, but Quanah wanted very much to have her exhumed and reinterred in the cemetery at Post Oak Mission, which was near his home. He also wanted to be buried there. Using his long-standing influence and friendship with the Texas and Oklahoma legislatures, he was able to secure the funds necessary for the operation. In October of 1910, Quanah stood in the Post Oak cemetery and watched his mother's casket slowly lowered into the ground.

The following February, Quanah Parker became ill and attended a healing ceremony on the Cheyenne reservation. The ceremony seemed to have had no effect because his condition worsened soon after. Following several weeks of illness, Quanah passed away on February 23, 1911. He died as an Indian. As he was breathing his last, the puhakut who was in attendance, prayed: "Father in heaven, this, our brother, is coming." Then, he embraced Quanah, flapped his arms, and imitated an eagle's call. Within moments, the Serpent Eagle flew the earth.

A pensive Quanah. Investigating reservation unrest in 1903, a government official reported that "Quanah would have been a leader and governor in any circle where fate might have cast him—it is in his blood."

Quanah was buried next to his mother in Post Oak cemetery. The U.S. government paid for a red-granite gravestone for Quanah, on which was inscribed, "Resting here until day breaks and shadows fall and darkness disappears." He was the last principal chief of the Comanches. Only Congress could appoint another, and they chose not to do so.

That more than 1,000 people—both Indian and non-Indian—attended his funeral is a tribute to Quanah Parker's abilities to thrive in two worlds. Others had chosen to ignore reality but he was ever practical. Quanah recognized from the start that the Indians were at a great disadvantage among the growing number of whites in their new surroundings. The only way for the Indians to survive was to adapt to those aspects of mainstream American culture that were most important to the government officials. By doing so, the Indians could use those concessions as bargaining tools when other aspects of their culture were threatened. Throughout his life, Quanah Parker was able to discern what had to be sacrificed in order to preserve what could be retained.

CHRONOLOGY

ca. 1845	Born in what is now east-central Texas
1859	Mother, Cynthia Ann Parker (Naduah), and sister, Topsannah, taken captive by U.S. Army
1861	Father, Peta Nokona, dies from wounds received during a raid against the Apaches; Quanah goes to live among the Kotsoteka Comanches
1862	Goes to live among the Quahadi Comanches
1866	Elopes with first wife, Weckeah, and forms his own band
1867	Rejoins the Quahadis, along with his rebel warriors and Weckeah
1871	Engages in first battle with Colonel Ranald Mackenzie and his U.S. military forces
1874	Participates in unsuccessful Indian attack on Adobe Walls trading post
1875	Surrenders, with rest of the Quahadi band, to Colonel Mackenzie at Fort Sill in Indian Territory
1884	Leads Indian delegation to Washington, D.C., to argue for the leasing of reservation land to cattlemen
1885	Leads second delegation to Washington
1887	Successfully lobbies to delay allotment of the Comanche, Kiowa, and Kiowa-Apache reservation
1891	Heads a third proleasing delegation
1892–1900	Heads three anti-allotment delegations to Washington
1904	Appointed assistant farmer for the Comanche, Kiowa, and Kiowa-Apache reservation
1905	Serves as one of five American Indian representatives at the inauguration of President Theodore Roosevelt
1910	Takes part in opening of the town of Quanah and the Quanah, Acme, and Pacific Railroad, both in Texas; successfully lobbies to have his mother's remains exhumed and reinterred at Post Oak Mission cemetery near his home
1911	Dies on February 23 and is buried next to his mother

FURTHER READING

Fehrenbach, T. R. *Comanches: The Destruction of a People*. New York: Knopf, 1974.

Hagan, William T. *United States–Comanche Relations: The Reservation Years*. New Haven: Yale University Press, 1976.

Hilts, Len. *Quanah Parker*. New York: Harcourt Brace Jovanovich, 1987.

Jackson, Clyde L., and Grace Jackson. *Quanah Parker: Last Chief of the Comanches*. New York: Exposition Press, 1963.

Rollings, Willard H. *The Comanche*. New York: Chelsea House, 1989.

Tilghman, Zoe A. *Quanah: The Eagle of the Comanches*. Oklahoma City: Harlow, 1938.

Wallace, Earnest, and E. Adamson Hoebel. *The Comanches: Lords of the Southern Plains*. Norman: University of Oklahoma Press, 1952.

Weems, John Edward. *Death Song: The Last of the Indian Wars*. Garden City, NY: Doubleday, 1976.

INDEX

PICTURE CREDITS

Archives Division, Texas State Library, pages 52–53, 55; Drawing by George Catlin, courtesy of New-York Historical Society, page 39; Colorado Historical Society, page 34 (#F 32518); From *Cynthia Ann Parker* by James de Shields, New York Public Library, Astor, Lenox and Tilden Foundations, page 104; Courtesy of Department of Library Services, American Museum of Natural History, photo by Irving Dutcher, page 62 (#312296); Courtesy of Department of Library Services, American Museum of Natural History, photo by H. S. Rice, page 28 (#312926); Courtesy of Fort Sill Museum, pages 10, 64, 68, 78, 95, 100, 103; Courtesy of Kansas State Historical Society, Topeka, page 3; Library of Congress, pages 32–33, 71 (#934); Museum of New Mexico, page 30 (#50828); Courtesy of National Museum of the American Indian, Smithsonian Institution, page 89 (#31639); Courtesy of Oklahoma Historical Society, page 99 (#2512); Courtesy of Panhandle Plains Historical Society, Canyon, Texas, pages 17, 76; Smithsonian Institution, National Anthropological Archives, pages 106 (neg # 1746-A-2), 20 (neg. # 1669), 25 (neg. # 1564), 40 (neg. # 38709), 41 (neg. # 20501K), 42, 56 (neg. # 1205), 66 (neg. # 55947), 69 (neg. # 1741A), 74 (neg. # 1746-C-2), 83 (neg. # 4195), 86–87 (neg. # 1778A), 92 (neg. # 50322), 96 (neg. # 1749-A); Photo by W. S. Soule, Barker Texas History Center, the University of Texas at Austin, page 50; Stanton, TW 1109 US Geological Survey for the Brazos River, page 13; University of Texas at San Antonio, Institute of Texan Cultures, pages 26 (# 68-2019), 36–37 (# 68-67), 46 (# 68-172), 48 (# 80-7), 58 (# 83-375), 59 (# 73-152), 73 (# 75-299), Western History Collections, University of Oklahoma Library, pages 15, 44, 60, 81, 85.

Map (page 23) by Gary Tong.

CLAIRE WILSON lives in New York City, where she works as an editor and a freelance writer. She holds a B.A. in anthropology from CUNY/Queens College and completed two years of graduate work, also in anthropology, at the State University of New York at Binghamton. She developed a deep interest in the life and history of American Indian peoples during both her studies and her work on the INDIANS OF NORTH AMERICA series at Chelsea House Publishers.

W. DAVID BAIRD is the Howard A. White Professor of History at Pepperdine University in Malibu, California. He holds a Ph.D. from the University of Oklahoma and was formerly on the faculty of history at the University of Arkansas, Fayetteville, and Oklahoma State University. He has served as president of both the Western History Association, a professional organization, and Phi Alpha Theta, the international honor society for students of history. Dr. Baird is also the author of *The Quapaw Indians: A History of the Downstream People* and *Peter Pitchlynn: Chief of the Choctaws* and the editor of *A Creek Warrior of the Confederacy: The Autobiography of Chief G. W. Grayson.*